MASTERING
FERMENTATION

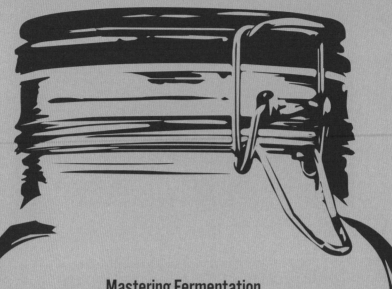

Mastering Fermentation

13-Digit ISBN: 978-1-64643-421-3
10-Digit ISBN: 1-64643-421-8

This book may be ordered by mail from the publisher. Please include $5.99 for postage and handling.

Please support your local bookseller first!

Books published by Cider Mill Press Book Publishers are available at special discounts for bulk purchases in the United States by corporations, institutions, and other organizations. For more information, please contact the publisher.

Cider Mill Press Book Publishers
"Where good books are ready for press"
501 Nelson Place
Nashville, Tennessee 37214

cidermillpress.com

Typography: Alternate Gothic 1, Ballinger
Image Credits: Pages 25, 26, 29, 30, 34, 48, and 161 courtesy of Cider Mill Press. All other photos used under official license from Shutterstock.com.

Printed in India

23 24 25 26 27 REP 5 4 3 2 1

First Edition

MASTERING FERMENTATION

75+ HOMEMADE RECIPES FOR SUSTAINABLE LIVING

KEITH SARASIN

CIDER MILL PRESS

BOOK PUBLISHERS

Contents

Introduction

The ancient technique of fermentation has been used to preserve food and improve both its flavor and nutritional content for thousands of years. This book is a thorough examination of the process, looking at the numerous types of fermentation, including acetic acid, lactic acid, and alcoholic fermentation, the science that supports it, and the equipment and methods used in the practice of it.

To get there, I will break down the fermenting process for a wide range of foods, from traditional favorites like sauerkraut and kimchi to more unusual fermented foods like kefir, kombucha, hot sauces, and South Indian staples such as dosa. Following the careful, clear directions in each preparation will have you feeling comfortable with fermentation in no time, allowing you to confidently prepare healthy and delicious fermented foods.

I also cover how to deal with problems frequently encountered during fermentation, like mold and unpleasant flavors. Sticking to the guidelines provided, you'll be able to better understand the process, and either avoid these issues entirely, or remedy them effectively.

In short, fermenting is a necessary pursuit for the passionate home cook, helping to cut down on waste, improve flavor, and produce nutrients that aid digestion and support a healthy gut. This book will set you on the path to take advantage of all these benefits, all from the comfort of your home.

A Brief History of Fermentation

For thousands of years, societies around the world have used fermentation to preserve food, with the earliest recorded instances of fermentation occurring in ancient Mesopotamia and Egypt, where grains and fruits were fermented to produce beer and wine, circa 6000 BCE.

But the practice was not limited to the Fertile Crescent. Ancient Chinese, Indian, and Greek cultures all employed fermentation—soybeans were fermented in China to produce tofu and soy sauce; pickles and yogurt were common fermented foods enjoyed in India; and olives were fermented in Greece to create the olive oil the peninsula is famed for.

In the Middle Ages, fermentation was an essential technique, producing the alcoholic beverages that were often safer to consume than water, as well as staples like cheese and pickles.

Louis Pasteur's nineteenth-century discovery that microbes are what enable fermentation improved our understanding of the procedure. New kinds of fermented foods were created as a result, including bread and commercial yogurt.

During the twentieth century, fermentation techniques continued to advance thanks to the development of technologies like pasteurization and refrigeration, and it remains a common method of food production today.

Fermentated foods have also been crucial to introducing people to numerous cuisines from all over the world. For instance, fermentation is used in Korea to create traditional foods like kimchi, a dish featuring spicy cabbage that is suddenly everywhere. Miso, soy sauce, and sake are a few examples of fermented Japanese foods that are popular all over the world.

Fermenting vs. Pickling

Two techniques for preserving food and imparting taste are fermentation and pickling. The method they use to produce their signature sour flavors provides the fundamental difference between them. In pickling, immersing food in an acidic liquid imparts the sour taste, whereas fermentation is a metabolic process performed by enzymes, bacteria, or yeast in an anaerobic (low-oxygen) environment. This process releases a series of by-products, including acetic acid, lactic acid, alcohol, and carbon dioxide.

Natural fermentation usually takes longer than pickling to preserve food, in some cases requiring weeks or months. On the other hand, preservation through pickling can be accomplished in a few hours or days. But that speed comes at a cost, as pickled foods lack the nuanced, complex flavors that are developed through the wide range of acids and chemicals produced during fermentation. Pickled foods will also not support general gut health as well as fermented foods, as the high amounts of acid required to pickle something keep probiotic microorganisms such as lactobacilli and bifidobacteria in check.

Another distinction is that, while pickling is most often done with vegetables and fruits, fermentation can be done with a wide range of food, including grains and dairy products, which become easier to digest after undergoing fermentation.

Basic Tools

You don't need too much to start fermenting at home, but the following equipment, sterilized before each use, is a must:

- **A sizable glass jar or crock with a tight-fitting lid.** Make sure the jar or crock you select can hold all of your ingredients when fermenting.

- **A fermentation weight.** This small weight is placed on top of the food to keep it submerged and prevent the growth of mold. Use a fermentation weight that has been specifically created for the purpose, or a sterilized, heavy object like a small glass jar filled with water.

- **Clean cheesecloth.** Place this at the top of the jar to keep out dust and other particles.

- Rubber bands. Use this to secure the cheesecloth in place.

- **An instant-read thermometer.** Monitoring the temperature of your fermentation is essential for ensuring that it is proceeding at the proper rate and doesn't spoil.

- **A pH meter or pH strips.** These will monitor the acidity of whatever is fermenting, another crucial element to determine whether it is fermenting properly.

- **A kitchen scale, measuring cups, and measuring spoons.** Being precise when fermenting is crucial, and these implements allow you to make sure all of the ratios in a preparation are on point.

- **Cutting boards, knives, and spoons.** These implements are necessary to properly prepare and handle the ingredients.

Storing Fermented Foods

In order to get all of the benefits that fermented foods offer, it's crucial to store them properly to keep them safe and fresh. Following are some suggestions for preserving fermented foods:

- **Refrigerate them:** To slow down fermentation and stop the formation of hazardous bacteria, fermented foods should be kept in the refrigerator at a temperature of 35°F to 40°F.

- **Use airtight containers:** To prevent bacterial contamination from other foods in the refrigerator and to prevent the food from drying out, fermented foods should be stored in airtight containers. A nice choice is glass jars with tight-fitting lids.

- **Burp the jars:** Gases created during fermentation might cause pressure to increase inside the jar. Make sure to "burp" the jar every day by slightly opening the lid to let the gas out.

- **Examine the fermented food frequently for mold,** which can be identified by a white, blue, or black discoloration on the surface. If mold is present, throw away the entire batch since it may spread to other components of the food.

- **The best way to store fermented foods** is in small amounts that can be consumed within a few weeks. This makes it more likely to stay fresh and not spoil before you can consume it.

- **Keep fermented foods in a cold, dark location:** If you're storing them for an extended period of time, it's best to keep them in a root cellar, garage, or pantry. By doing so, the food will be preserved and the fermentation process will be slowed.

These recommendations will help you preserve the freshness and safety of your fermented foods for as long as possible. Always use your senses—taste, smell, and sight—to determine whether the fermented food is still safe to consume. It is preferable to throw something away if it seems off than to run the danger of being ill.

Canning

When I talk about fermentation, people frequently exclaim, "Cool! Canning's something I've always wanted to attempt." Prior to learning about fermenting food, I also mistakenly believed that the phrases "fermenting" and "canning" meant the same thing. In truth, they couldn't be more different.

In order to preserve food via canning, that food must be sealed in an airtight container and heated to a high temperature in order to destroy any bacteria or other germs that may be present. Contrast that to fermentation, which instead puts some of those microorganisms canning seeks to eliminate to work, creating an environment that is hostile to hazardous bacteria.

Proper canning helps you preserve the flavors of the seasons. Fermentation also enables preservation, but the flavors of what is preserved will be altered, and the nutritional content improved.

Still, there will be instances where you may want to can some of the jams and other items you've produced through fermentation, in order to provide them with a longer shelf life. Just be aware that canning is not the best method for preserving fermented foods, as the good bacteria they contain are often lost when exposed to extreme heat. The best way to preserve your fermentations is to move fermented items to cold storage, such as a refrigerator or cold cellar, if you really want to retain their most beneficial qualities.

To can an item, bring a pot of water to a boil. Place your mason jars in the water for 15 to 20 minutes to sterilize them. Do not boil the mason jar lids, as this may prevent them from creating a proper seal when the time comes.

Bring water to a boil in the large canning pot. Fill the sterilized mason jars with whatever you are canning. Place the lids on the jars and secure the bands tightly. Place the jars in the boiling water for 40 minutes. Use a pair of canning tongs to remove the jars from the boiling water and let them cool. As they are cooling, you should hear the classic "ping and pop" sound of the lids creating a seal.

After 6 hours, check the lids. There should be no give in them and they should be suctioned onto the jars. Discard any lids and food that did not seal properly.

Notes on Safety

Food fermentation is a fantastic method to add taste and nutrition to your diet, but it's crucial to practice safety when doing so. The following advice can help you stay safe while fermenting food:

- **Use clean equipment:** Before you begin fermenting, make sure that all of your equipment has been sterilized and is clear of any debris or bacteria.

- **Ensure complete coverage:** To keep impurities from contaminating your fermented food, keep it covered with a fresh cloth or lid.

- **Use the correct salt:** To ferment your food, use a high-quality noniodized salt. The beneficial bacteria can be inhibited by the iodine in iodized salt.

- **Use fresh ingredients:** When fermenting food, only use fresh, high-quality ingredients. Any ingredients that have mold or are spoiled should not be used.

- **Keep the fermentation temperature within the proper range:** The growth of beneficial bacteria depends on fermentation occurring at the proper temperature. The majority of fermentation occurs at room temperature (68°F to 72°F).

- **Be mindful of the typical fermentation period:** Fermented foods require different amounts of time to ferment, so be sure to stick to the particular recipe and check in on the preparation regularly to make sure it's not taking too long.

- **Throw away any rotten or moldy food:** If you discover any mold or deterioration on your fermented food, discard it immediately and resume with a sterilized jar.

By following these suggestions, you can ensure that your fermented foods are safe to eat. Although fermentation is a natural process, it's crucial to be always remain aware of the environment it is occurring in, and to keep an eye out for indicators of spoiling or mold development. When in doubt, throw it out.

Sourdough

Both yeasts and lactic acid bacteria are elements of fermentation commonly found in sourdough cultures. There can be substantial variations between one culture and another, especially if the cultures originated in different geographical areas, due to the number of different wild yeasts and lactic acid bacteria that can populate a sourdough culture.

Thanks to the rich microcosmos of living fungi and bacteria, making sourdough bread includes both alcoholic and lactic fermentation processes. The baked breads will differ considerably in terms of volume, texture, and flavor depending on the specific type of sourdough culture used and the way the culture is kept.

When a sourdough culture is stable and capable of rising a dough, it is called sourdough starter.

When a sourdough starter is heavily neglected, yeast populations become very small and the type of lactic acid bacteria that produces acetic acid will become prevalent, giving us a very sour bread with poor volume development.

On the other hand, a sourdough culture that pullulates yeast and has a predominance of heterofermentative lactic acid bacteria will reward our careful attention by producing a well-developed loaf, with ideal volume and texture, in which flavor is complex but not acidic.

All doughs made with sourdough as the rising agent are based on the indirect method of fermentation. To use sourdough in a dough, one needs an active sourdough starter that has been recently fed water and flour. As with yeast-based preferments, fermentation time in sourdough-based baking is determined by the relative amount of sourdough added to the mixture of flour and water ahead of adding it to the final dough.

Scientific evidence shows bread made with sourdough is more digestible as compared to bread made with baker's yeast. This is due to two main reasons: time and lactic fermentation. Regarding time, fermentation with sourdough is generally longer than a yeast-based dough, because in sourdough baking it is neither possible to use the direct method, nor to shorten final fermentation time below a minimum of 3 to 4 hours. It must be said that yeasted breads using preferments have some of the good characteristics of sourdough.

The second "superpower" of sourdough is lactic fermentation. While it does not help to rise the dough, it does plenty to make it more gut friendly. The processes involved are complex, but the main point is simple: lactic fermentation is superior to alcoholic fermentation in catabolizing proteins, such as gluten, which are potentially problematic for our digestive system.

HOW TO MAKE A STARTER

It is possible to get a starter from a friend or to buy it online from trusted sellers. However, making your own starter is a highly rewarding endeavor that you do not want to miss out on. Once a stable starter has been created, it can be maintained indefinitely, assuming it receives proper care. There are several ways to create a starter. The most straightforward method is to make use of the many wild yeasts and good bacteria naturally occurring in flour and in the air, and allow time to do the rest.

Day 1, Morning

30 g lukewarm water (around 80°F)
6 g whole-grain rye flour
24 g all-purpose flour

Mix the ingredients together and put the mixture in a washed and rinsed container, making sure that the mixture takes up no more than one-third of the container. Put the lid on (if you are using a glass jar, do not screw the lid). Place the container in a naturally warm (but not hot) spot. Ideally, the temperature should be around 80°F, so if you do not have a place in your home that gets this warm, consider investing in an incubator.

You may also want to use bottled water to create a starter, because chemicals in tap water could inhibit the starter's development in the early stages.

Day 2, Morning

30 g of your starter from the day before
30 g lukewarm water
6 g whole-grain rye flour
24 g all-purpose flour

Discard the rest of your starter. Add the water and mix. Then add the flours, mix, and scrape the walls of the container well to keep it clean. Place the container back in the warm spot.

Day 2, Evening

30 g of your starter from the morning
30 g lukewarm water
6 g whole-grain rye flour
24 g all-purpose flour

Discard the rest of your starter. Add the water and mix. Then add the flours, mix, and scrape the walls of the container well to keep it clean. Place the container back in the warm spot.

At this point, you should be seeing some signs of life, some activity, which will manifest itself as bubbles.

Day 3, 4, 5, and So On

Continue to do what was described for Day 2, until your starter can double itself within 12 hours, is all bubbly, and smells good (not too acidic, the aroma of a healthy starter is similar to a freshly cut green apple). Make sure that the color stays within the yellow-brown shades, and does not take any orange or blueish tone.

By Day 6 or 7, you may have successfully created a starter. Does it double in 12 hours? Does it smell sweet and is it full of bubbles? If the answer is no, then continue as in the previous days. Hopefully, your sourdough culture will soon come to life, but if it does not, discard and start over.

If instead you have given birth to a stable sourdough culture, the task now is keeping it healthy. You have two main options for how to maintain your sourdough starter: either refrigerating the starter, or keeping it at room temperature.

HOW TO MAINTAIN A SOURDOUGH STARTER

If you just started a sourdough culture, it is not recommended to shift to refrigerated maintenance for a few weeks. During those first few weeks at room temperature, strains of yeast and bacteria that are optimal for bread baking will be selected. Once the culture is stable, periods of refrigeration will not disrupt its main composition. Of course, this all depends on how good you are at feeding your starter at the right time.

When keeping the starter at room temperature, it is ideal to feed it once every 12 hours. In the beginning, use the same amount of starter, water, and flour, in a 1:1:1 ratio for each feeding. This means that every 12 hours you will take some of your starter and combine it with equal amounts of water and flour (in terms of weight, not volume). The remaining starter can be discarded or used for other preparations.

After several days at room temperature, your starter should become very active and you will need to change the ratio. The relative amounts for your feedings could then become, for instance, 1:2:2. This means that you will use half the amount of starter, keeping the same amounts of water and flour. What matters is that the hydration (the proportion of water to flour) remains constant. The amount of starter from the previous feeding can instead change depending on how active the starter is from day to day, how warm the place where you are storing the starter is, and how capable you are of doing two feedings a day. If you want to feed your starter only once a day, you can inoculate a small amount of starter in your mixture of water and flour.

When your sourdough culture has stabilized, you can make life easier by alternating between leaving the starter unfed in the fridge, and bringing it to room temperature, feeding as described previously.

Ideally, you want to leave the starter unfed in the fridge for no more than 5 days, and then feed it at room temperature at least three times before putting the starter, just fed, back into the fridge.

Always choose the least cold spot of your fridge to keep your starter, and make sure the overall temperature of the fridge does not go below 36°F.

Although not optimal, if it does happen that you leave your starter unfed in the refrigerator for a prolonged amount of time, do not worry.

It takes a very long time to kill a stable sourdough culture. If this occurs, let your sourdough starter stay at room temperature longer, with repeated feedings, to regenerate all of the yeast cells and the good bacteria.

Sourdough Bread

A foundational recipe that will have the tangy taste and crispy crust everyone wants from a sourdough loaf.

1 cup water, at room temperature

3⅓ cups bread flour, plus more as needed

⅓ cup whole wheat flour

1 cup Sourdough Starter (see page 18)

2 teaspoons kosher salt

1. Place the water and flours in the work bowl of a stand mixer fitted with the dough hook and work the mixture at low speed for 6 minutes. Remove the bowl from the mixer and cover it with plastic wrap. Let the dough sit at room temperature for 1 hour to allow the dough to autolyse.

2. Place the work bowl back on the mixer and add the starter and salt. Knead the mixture at low speed until the dough starts to come together, about 2 minutes. Increase the speed to medium and knead until the dough is elastic and pulls away from the side of the bowl.

3. Dust a 9-inch banneton (proofing basket) with flour. Shape the dough into a ball and place it in the proofing basket, seam side down. Cover the bread with plastic wrap and let it sit on the counter for 2 hours.

4. Place the basket in the refrigerator and let it rest overnight.

5. Preheat the oven to 450°F and place a baking stone on a rack positioned in the middle.

6. Dust a peel with flour and gently turn the bread onto the peel so that the seam is facing up.

7. With a very sharp knife, carefully score the dough just off center. Make sure the knife is at a 45-degree angle to the dough.

8. Gently slide the sourdough onto the baking stone. Spray the oven with 5 spritzes of water and bake the bread for 20 minutes.

9. Open the oven, spray the oven with 5 more spritzes of water, and bake the bread until the crust is golden brown, about 20 minutes. The internal temperature of the bread should be at least 210°F. Remove the bread from the oven, place it on a wire rack, and let it cool completely before slicing.

Summer Berry Sourdough

Once your freezer is filled up with the fruits of your summer labors, this is a wonderful spot for some of your berry-picking haul.

1 cup water, at room temperature

3⅓ cups bread flour, plus more as needed

⅓ cup whole wheat flour

2 tablespoons lavender buds

¼ cup frozen blueberries

¼ cup frozen raspberries

¼ cup frozen blackberries

1 cup Sourdough Starter (see page 18)

2 teaspoons kosher salt

1. Place the water, flours, and lavender in the work bowl of a stand mixer fitted with the dough hook and work the mixture on low for 6 minutes. Remove the bowl from the mixer and cover it with plastic wrap. Let the dough sit at room temperature for 1 hour to allow the dough to autolyse.

2. Place the work bowl back on the mixer and add the berries, starter, and salt. Knead the mixture at low speed until the dough starts to come together, about 2 minutes. Increase the speed to medium and knead until the dough is elastic and pulls away from the side of the bowl.

3. Shape the dough into a ball and spray the seam side with water. Dust a 9-inch banneton (proofing basket) with bread flour. Place the dough in the proofing basket, seam side down. Cover the bread with plastic wrap and let it sit on the counter for 2 hours.

4. Place the basket in the refrigerator and let it rest overnight.

5. Preheat the oven to 450°F and place a baking stone on a rack positioned in the middle.

6. Dust a peel with bread flour and gently turn the bread onto the peel so that the seam is facing up.

7. With a very sharp knife, carefully score the dough just off center. Make sure the knife is at a 45-degree angle to the dough.

8. Gently slide the sourdough onto the baking stone. Spray the oven with 5 spritzes of water and bake the bread for 20 minutes.

9. Open the oven, spray the oven with 5 more spritzes of water, and bake the bread until the crust is golden brown, about 20 minutes. The internal temperature of the bread should be at least 210°F when it is ready.

10. Remove the bread from the oven, place it on a wire rack, and let it cool completely before slicing.

Yield: 1 Loaf / **Active Time:** 1 Hour and 30 Minutes / **Total Time:** 24 Hours

Wild Blueberry Sourdough Bread

If you're craving French toast, make this sourdough the night before.

1 cup water, at room temperature

3⅓ cups bread flour, plus more as needed

⅓ cup whole wheat flour

½ cup frozen wild blueberries

½ cup dried blueberries

1 cup Sourdough Starter (see page 18)

2 teaspoons kosher salt

1. Place the water and flours in the work bowl of a stand mixer fitted with the dough hook and work the mixture on low for 6 minutes. Remove the bowl from the mixer and cover it with plastic wrap. Let the dough sit at room temperature for 1 hour to allow the dough to autolyse.

2. Place the work bowl back on the mixer and add the berries, starter, and salt. Knead the mixture at low speed until the dough starts to come together, about 2 minutes. Increase the speed to medium and knead until the dough is elastic and pulls away from the side of the bowl.

3. Shape the dough into a ball and spray the seam side with water. Dust a 9-inch banneton (proofing basket) with bread flour. Place the dough in the proofing basket, seam side down. Cover the bread with plastic wrap and let it sit on the counter for 2 hours.

4. Place the basket in the refrigerator and let it rest overnight.

5. Preheat the oven to 450°F and place a baking stone on a rack positioned in the middle.

6. Dust a peel with bread flour and gently turn the bread onto the peel so that the seam is facing up.

7. With a very sharp knife, carefully score the dough just off center. Make sure the knife is at a 45-degree angle to the dough.

8. Gently slide the sourdough onto the baking stone. Spray the oven with 5 spritzes of water and bake the bread for 20 minutes.

9. Open the oven, spray the oven with 5 more spritzes of water, and bake the bread until the crust is golden brown, about 20 minutes. The internal temperature of the bread should be at least 210°F when it is ready.

10. Remove the bread from the oven, place it on a wire rack, and let it cool completely before slicing.

Black Sesame Sourdough Bread

Black tahini lends this bread plenty of earthiness, plus an eye-catching look.

1 cup water, at room temperature

3⅓ cups bread flour, plus more as needed

⅓ cup whole wheat flour

½ cup black tahini paste

1 cup Sourdough Starter (see page 18)

2 teaspoons kosher salt

1 cup black sesame seeds

1. Place the water and flours in the work bowl of a stand mixer fitted with the dough hook and work the mixture at low speed for 6 minutes. Remove the bowl from the mixer and cover it with plastic wrap. Let the dough sit at room temperature for 1 hour to allow the dough to autolyse.

2. Place the work bowl back on the mixer and add the black tahini paste, starter, and salt. Knead the mixture at low speed until the dough starts to come together, about 2 minutes. Increase the speed to medium and knead until the dough is elastic and pulls away from the side of the bowl.

3. Place the sesame seeds on a plate. Shape the dough into a ball and spray the seam side with water. Roll the top of the dough in the sesame seeds until coated.

4. Dust a 9-inch banneton (proofing basket) with flour. Place the dough in the proofing basket, seeded side down. Cover the bread with plastic wrap and let it sit on the counter for 2 hours.

5. Place the basket in the refrigerator and let it rest overnight.

6. Preheat the oven to 450°F and place a baking stone on a rack positioned in the middle.

7. Dust a peel with flour and gently turn the bread onto the peel so that the seeded side is facing up.

8. With a very sharp knife, carefully score the dough just off center. Make sure the knife is at a 45-degree angle to the dough.

9. Gently slide the sourdough onto the baking stone. Spray the oven with 5 spritzes of water and bake the bread for 20 minutes.

10. Open the oven, spray the oven with 5 more spritzes of water, and bake the bread until the crust is golden brown, about 20 minutes. The internal temperature of the bread should be at least 210°F. Remove the bread from the oven, place it on a wire rack, and let it cool completely before slicing.

Yield: 1 Loaf / **Active Time:** 1 Hour and 30 Minutes / **Total Time:** 24 Hours

Harvest Sourdough Bread

Good in just about any situation, but sublime as the base of a sandwich filled with Thanksgiving leftovers.

1 cup water, at room temperature

3⅓ cups bread flour, plus more as needed

⅓ cup whole wheat flour

¼ cup dried cranberries

2 tablespoons pumpkin seeds, plus more for topping

2 tablespoons sunflower seeds, plus more for topping

2 tablespoons poppy seeds, plus more for topping

2 tablespoons chia seeds, plus more for topping

1 cup Sourdough Starter (see page 18)

2 teaspoons kosher salt

1. Place the water and flours in the work bowl of a stand mixer fitted with the dough hook and work the mixture on low for 6 minutes. Remove the bowl from the mixer and cover it with plastic wrap. Let the dough sit at room temperature for 1 hour to allow the dough to autolyse.

2. Place the work bowl back on the mixer and add the cranberries, seeds, starter, and salt. Knead the mixture at low speed until the dough starts to come together, about 2 minutes. Increase the speed to medium and knead until the dough is elastic and pulls away from the side of the bowl.

3. Combine the seeds for topping on a plate. Shape the dough into a ball and spray the seam side with water. Roll the top of the dough in the mixture until coated.

4. Dust a 9-inch banneton (proofing basket) with bread flour. Place the dough in the proofing basket, seeded side down. Cover the bread with plastic wrap and let it sit on the counter for 2 hours.

5. Place the basket in the refrigerator and let it rest overnight.

6. Preheat the oven to 450°F and place a baking stone on a rack positioned in the middle.

7. Dust a peel with bread flour and gently turn the bread onto the peel so that the seeded side is facing up.

8. With a very sharp knife, carefully score the dough just off center. Make sure the knife is at a 45-degree angle to the dough.

9. Gently slide the sourdough onto the baking stone. Spray the oven with 5 spritzes of water and bake the bread for 20 minutes.

10. Open the oven, spray the oven with 5 more spritzes of water, and bake the bread until the crust is golden brown, about 20 minutes. The internal temperature of the bread should be at least 210°F.

11. Remove the bread from the oven, place it on a wire rack, and let it cool completely before slicing.

Multigrain Sourdough Bread

The texture provided by the oats and seeds is the drawing card here.

1 cup water, at room temperature

3⅓ cups bread flour, plus more as needed

⅓ cup whole wheat flour

1 cup rolled oats, plus more for topping

¼ cup sunflower seeds

¼ cup millet seeds

1 cup Sourdough Starter (see page 18)

2 teaspoons kosher salt

1. Place the water and flours in the work bowl of a stand mixer fitted with the dough hook and work the mixture on low for 6 minutes. Remove the bowl from the mixer and cover it with plastic wrap. Let the dough sit at room temperature for 1 hour to allow the dough to autolyse.

2. Place the work bowl back on the mixer and add the oats, seeds, starter, and salt. Knead the mixture at low speed until the dough starts to come together, about 2 minutes. Increase the speed to medium and knead until the dough is elastic and pulls away from the side of the bowl.

3. Place more oats on a plate. Shape the dough into a ball and spray the seam side with water. Roll the top of the dough in the oats until coated.

4. Dust a 9-inch banneton (proofing basket) with bread flour. Place the dough in the proofing basket, oat side down. Cover the bread with plastic wrap and let it sit on the counter for 2 hours.

5. Place the basket in the refrigerator and let it rest overnight.

6. Preheat the oven to 450°F and place a baking stone on a rack positioned in the middle.

7. Dust a peel with bread flour and gently turn the bread onto the peel so that the oat side is facing up.

8. With a very sharp knife, carefully score the dough just off center. Make sure the knife is at a 45-degree angle to the dough.

9. Gently slide the sourdough onto the baking stone. Spray the oven with 5 spritzes of water and bake the bread for 20 minutes.

10. Open the oven, spray the oven with 5 more spritzes of water, and bake the bread until the crust is golden brown, about 20 minutes. The internal temperature of the bread should be at least 210°F.

11. Remove the bread from the oven, place it on a wire rack, and let it cool completely before slicing.

Blue Pea Flower Sourdough Bread

Due to the high acidity of sourdough, the blue pea flower powder will actually produce a loaf that is closer to purple. It's a unique bread—both in terms of looks and taste.

1 cup water, at room temperature

3⅓ cups bread flour, plus more as needed

⅓ cup whole wheat flour

¼ cup blue pea flower powder

1 cup Sourdough Starter (see page 18)

2 teaspoons kosher salt

1. Place the water, flours, and blue pea flower powder in the work bowl of a stand mixer fitted with the dough hook and work the mixture at low speed for 6 minutes. Remove the bowl from the mixer and cover it with plastic wrap. Let the dough sit at room temperature for 1 hour to allow the dough to autolyse.

2. Place the work bowl back on the mixer and add the starter and salt. Knead the mixture at low speed until the dough starts to come together, about 2 minutes. Increase the speed to medium and knead until the dough is elastic and pulls away from the side of the bowl.

3. Shape the dough into a ball and spray the seam side with water. Dust a 9-inch banneton (proofing basket) with flour. Place the dough in the proofing basket, seam side down. Cover the bread with plastic wrap and let it sit on the counter for 2 hours.

4. Place the basket in the refrigerator and let it rest overnight.

5. Preheat the oven to 450°F and place a baking stone on a rack positioned in the middle.

6. Dust a peel with flour and gently turn the bread onto the peel so that the seam is facing up.

7. With a very sharp knife, carefully score the dough just off center. Make sure the knife is at a 45-degree angle to the dough.

8. Gently slide the sourdough onto the baking stone. Spray the oven with 5 spritzes of water and bake the bread for 20 minutes.

9. Open the oven, spray the oven with 5 more spritzes of water, and bake the bread until the crust is golden brown, about 20 minutes. The internal temperature of the bread should be at least 210°F.

10. Remove the bread from the oven, place it on a wire rack, and let it cool completely before slicing.

Sourdough Crackers

If you like, incorporate 2 to 3 tablespoons of herbs or seeds into this dough.

1 cup Sourdough Starter
(see page 18)

1 cup all-purpose flour, plus
more as needed

½ teaspoon fine sea salt

4 tablespoons unsalted
butter, softened

Extra-virgin olive oil, as
needed

Maldon sea salt, to taste

1. Place the starter, flour, fine sea salt, and butter in a mixing bowl and work the mixture until it comes together as a smooth dough.

2. Divide the dough in half and form each piece into a rectangle. Cover the dough in plastic wrap and chill in the refrigerator until it is firm, about 1 hour.

3. Preheat the oven to 350°F. Dust a piece of parchment paper and a rolling pin with flour. Place one piece of dough on the parchment paper and roll it out until it is about ⅟₁₆ inch thick.

4. Transfer the parchment paper, with the dough on it, to a baking sheet. Brush the dough with some olive oil and sprinkle the Maldon sea salt over the top.

5. Cut the crackers to the desired size and shape and prick each cracker with a fork. Repeat with the remaining piece of dough.

6. Place the crackers in the oven and bake until crispy and golden brown, 20 to 25 minutes, rotating the baking sheets halfway through.

7. Remove the crackers from the oven, place the baking sheets on wire racks, and let the crackers cool completely before enjoying.

Sourdough Pasta

This is the first of a handful of recipes Chef B. J. Beisler, one of my good friends, provided the project. I met B. J. about 5 years ago, when he was just a young sous chef at an incredible restaurant in New Hampshire, and even then I could tell that his passion and drive were unbelievable. I hosted a couple of pop-up dinners at the restaurant where B. J. worked, and eventually, we got around to talking about fermented food. Since that initial conversation, B. J. has taught me so much about fermentation, and how versatile it can be.

700 g all-purpose flour, plus more as needed

100 g Sourdough Starter (see page 18)

4 large eggs

100 g water

Pinch of fine sea salt, plus more to taste

Semolina flour, as needed

1. Weigh your ingredients, measuring the water in 2 containers—one should contain 60 grams of water, and the other 40 grams.

2. Place the all-purpose flour in a mixing bowl and make a small well in the middle. Add the Sourdough Starter and eggs and work the mixture with your hands until it starts holding together in clumps.

3. Add the 60 grams of water and the salt and work the mixture until it comes together as a shaggy dough. If the dough is too dry to hold together, add the remaining water in small increments until it does.

4. Remove the dough from the bowl and place it on an all-purpose flour–dusted work surface. Knead the dough until it is smooth, about 10 minutes. Cover the dough with plastic wrap and let it rest for 15 minutes.

5. Set up a station with a pasta maker, a sharp knife, parchment-lined baking sheets, a small bowl containing all-purpose flour, and another small bowl containing semolina flour.

6. Cut the dough into four pieces. Set the pasta machine to the widest setting and, working with one piece of dough at a time, run it through the machine, adjusting to a narrower setting with each pass, until it is the desired thickness (about ⅛ inch thick). Cut the rolled sheets of dough in half and dust them with all-purpose flour. Roll the sheets into logs and slice the dough into ¾-inch-wide strips. Cover the pieces of dough that you are not working on with plastic wrap, as it will prevent them from drying out.

7. Dust the cut pasta with semolina, shape them into bundles, and place them on the baking sheets.

8. Bring water to a boil in a large saucepan. Generously salt the water—it should taste like sea water. Add the pasta and stir it with a fork for 30 seconds. Cook until the pasta floats to the top, about 3 minutes. Drain and serve as desired.

Fruits & Veggies

We all know that Mother Nature is undefeated in terms of imbuing her products with unparalleled flavor and nutrition—when you bite into a fresh strawberry, for instance, it's hard to imagine that there are any levels above. As it turns out, there are, and fermentation is the code that allows you to access them.

By incorporating just a bit of friendly bacteria into the proceedings, the fruits and vegetables that key a proper diet become just a little bit better at performing the heavy lifting for a healthy lifestyle. From a handful of luscious jams to one of the fermentation world's heavy hitters, kimchi, which has the power to transform your entire palate, this chapter is loaded with wonderful ways to preserve the wonders of the natural world.

Spicy Pineapple

Another great recipe from my buddy and fermentation fanatic, B. J. Beisler. This can serve as a sweet-and-spicy base for sauces, or be enjoyed on its own.

1 whole pineapple, peeled and chopped

1 Fresno chile pepper, stem and seeds removed, sliced thin

Salt, as needed

1. Place a mixing bowl on a kitchen scale, tare it, and set the scale to measure grams.

2. Add the pineapple and chile to the bowl and weigh it.

3. Add 2 percent of the mixture's weight in salt to the bowl. Stir to combine and place the mixture and any liquid in a vacuum bag in a single layer, or in a mason jar. If using a mason jar, place a fermentation weight on top of the mixture and make sure that the solids are completely submerged.

4. Seal the container and place it in a dark, warm area until the flavor is to your liking, 2 to 4 days. Check the container every day to see if too much gas has built up. If it has, release the gas and reseal the container.

5. Remove the spicy pineapple from the container and either enjoy immediately or store in the refrigerator.

Raspberry Jam

This jam is perfect on toast, crackers, or as a filling for doughnuts.

1 pint of fresh raspberries

Salt, as needed

Agar agar powder, as needed

Water, as needed

1. Place a mixing bowl on a kitchen scale, tare it, and set the scale to measure grams.

2. Add the raspberries to the bowl and weigh them. Add 2 percent of the mixture's weight in salt to the bowl. Stir to combine and place the mixture and any liquid in a vacuum bag in a single layer, or in a mason jar. If using a mason jar, place a fermentation weight on top of the mixture and make sure that the solids are completely submerged, adding water as needed.

3. Seal the container and place it in a dark, warm area until the flavor is to your liking, 2 to 5 days. Check the container every day to see if too much gas has built up. If it has, release the gas and reseal the container.

4. Place a mixing bowl on a kitchen scale, tare it, and set the scale to measure grams. Place the fermented raspberries in a blender, puree until smooth, and strain the puree into the mixing bowl. Add 3 percent of the puree's weight in agar agar powder and stir until thoroughly combined.

5. Place the mixture in a small saucepan and slowly bring it to a boil, stirring continually to prevent the bottom from burning. Transfer the mixture to a baking pan and spread it into a thin, even layer. Place the mixture in the refrigerator and chill it until it has set.

6. Cut the set jam into cubes, place them in a blender, and puree until smooth, adding water as needed to get the desired consistency. Use immediately or store the jam in the refrigerator, where it will keep for up to 1 month. You can also can this jam, following the instructions on page 12.

Raspberry Jam

See page 43

Kimchi

A classic recipe that is a great place to begin your fermentation journey.

1 cup plus 1 tablespoon kosher salt

8 cups water, plus more as needed

7 lbs. napa cabbage, chopped

8 garlic cloves

2 oz. rice flour

1 onion

2 tablespoons minced shrimp

2-inch piece of fresh ginger root, grated

¼ cup fish sauce

2 lbs. daikon radish, peeled and cut into cubes

1 bunch of scallions, trimmed and chopped

½ cup gochugaru

1 tablespoon oyster sauce

2 Granny Smith apples, grated

1. Place 1 cup of salt and the water in a large pot and stir to combine. Add the cabbage and let it soak for 3 hours.

2. Place the garlic, rice flour, onion, and shrimp in a blender and puree until smooth. Transfer the mixture to a bowl.

3. Wearing rubber gloves, drain the cabbage, rinse it well, and add it to the bowl. Add the remaining ingredients, including the remaining salt, and work the mixture with your hands, looking to both squeeze as much liquid as possible from the cabbage and to combine the mixture.

4. Transfer the mixture to mason jars, pressing down to make sure the liquid covers the kimchi entirely. If the liquid does not cover the kimchi, add water as necessary.

5. Cover the jar with a paper towel and secure it with an elastic band. Store the kimchi in a cool, dark place until the flavor has developed to your liking, 2 to 4 days. Store in the refrigerator.

Yield: 6 Servings / **Active Time:** 30 Minutes / **Total Time:** 3 Days

Stuffed Cucumber Kimchi

This is a great recipe if you find yourself with a bumper crop of Kirby cucumbers, which are also known as pickling cucumbers.

10 Kirby cucumbers

3 tablespoons kosher salt

1 cup fresh chives, chopped (½-inch slices)

4 garlic cloves

1 teaspoon minced fresh ginger

¾ cup julienned carrots

½ cup thinly sliced yellow onion

½ cup gochugaru (Korean chili flakes)

1 tablespoon sugar

¼ cup water

1½ tablespoons minced saeujot (salted fermented shrimp)

1½ tablespoons fish sauce

1 tablespoon toasted sesame seeds

Water, as needed

1. Quarter each cucumber lengthwise, leaving ¼ inch at one end intact and connected.

2. Season the cucumbers with the salt, being sure to get inside each one. Place the cucumbers in a bowl, cover the bowl, and let the cucumbers sit for 1 hour.

3. Rinse the cucumbers with cold water and gently pat them dry.

4. Place the remaining ingredients in a bowl and stir until well combined.

5. Stuff the mixture into the cucumbers and then place the stuffed cucumbers in a mason jar, pressing down to make sure the liquid covers them entirely. If the liquid does not cover the stuffed cucumbers, add water as necessary. Let the jar sit in a warm, dark place for 24 hours.

6. Transfer the jar to the refrigerator and chill it for 2 days before enjoying the kimchi.

Lacto-Fermented Blueberries

My good friend B. J. had the good sense to intuit that the sweet-and-sour flavor of blueberries would become addictive when fermented. This preparation is as good on toast as it is on game meats.

1 pint of fresh blueberries

Salt, as needed

1. Place a mixing bowl on a kitchen scale, tare it, and set the scale to measure grams.

2. Pick over the blueberries, removing and discarding any rotten ones. Add the blueberries to the bowl and weigh them. Add 2 percent of the mixture's weight in salt to the bowl. Stir to combine and place the mixture and any liquid in a vacuum bag in a single layer, or in a mason jar. If using a mason jar, place a fermentation weight on top of the mixture and make sure that the solids are completely submerged, adding water as necessary.

3. Seal the container and place it in a dark, warm area until the flavor is to your liking, 2 to 5 days. Check the container every day to see if too much gas has built up. If it has, release the gas and reseal the container.

4. Briefly rinse the blueberries under cold water and either enjoy immediately or store in the refrigerator, where they will continue to ferment.

Blueberry & Chia Jam

Enjoy this on toasted slices of your favorite sourdough bread, or as a topping for yogurt or oatmeal. If you have a preference for a different berry, simply swap them in for the blueberries.

2 cups fresh or frozen blueberries

½ cup honey

2 tablespoons chia seeds

¼ cup water

2 tablespoons raw apple cider vinegar

1. Place the blueberries and honey in a medium saucepan and warm the mixture over medium heat, stirring occasionally, until the blueberries have released their juice and the mixture has thickened, 10 to 15 minutes.

2. While the blueberries and honey are warming in the pan, place the chia seeds and water in a bowl and let the mixture sit for 5 minutes so that it thickens and becomes gelatinous.

3. Stir the chia mixture and vinegar into the saucepan and then transfer the mixture into a clean, sterilized mason jar. Let the jam cool completely.

4. Seal the jar and store the jam in a cool, dark place until the flavor has developed to your liking, 3 to 5 days. Use immediately or store in the refrigerator for up to 1 month. You can also can this jam, following the instructions on page 12.

Blueberry & Chia Jam

See page 51

Sauerkraut

Sauerkraut is easy to prepare at home, and always hits the spot, whether you're looking for a snack that won't derail your quest to eat healthy, or looking to treat yourself with a reuben.

2 lb. head of cabbage

2 tablespoons fine sea salt

Water, as needed

1. Remove any wilted or damaged outer leaves from the cabbage. Cut the cabbage into quarters and remove the core. Slice the cabbage into thin shreds using a sharp knife or a mandoline.

2. Place the cabbage in a large bowl, add the salt, and massage the salt into the cabbage until the cabbage starts to release its liquid, about 5 minutes.

3. Transfer the cabbage and any liquid to a sterilized mason jar, pressing down firmly to remove any air pockets. The cabbage should be completely submerged in its own liquid. If it is not, add water as needed until the cabbage is submerged.

4. Seal the jar tightly and place the jar in a cool, dark place. Let it sit until the sauerkraut has a sour, tangy flavor and a crunchy texture, 3 to 4 weeks. Check the jar every few days to make sure the cabbage is still fully submerged and release any excess gas. If the sauerkraut is not tangy enough after 4 weeks, let it ferment for a few more weeks.

5. Use the sauerkraut immediately or store it in the refrigerator for up to 2 months.

Lacto-Fermented Carrots

With their slightly sour and crunchy texture, these carrots are a wonderful additional to a crudités platter, salads, or sandwiches.

4 cups peeled and grated carrots

2 tablespoons fine sea salt

Water, as needed

1. Place the grated carrots and salt in a bowl and massage the salt into the carrots until the carrots start to release their liquid, about 5 minutes.

2. Transfer the carrots and their liquid to a large, sterilized mason jar, pressing down firmly to remove any air pockets. The carrots should be completely submerged in their own liquid. If they are not, add water as needed until the carrots are submerged.

3. Seal the jar tightly and place it in a cool, dark place until the flavor of the carrots is slightly sour, and they have a slightly cloudy appearance, 3 to 4 weeks. Check the jar every few days day to make sure the carrots are fermenting properly—if you see any dark, moldy growth, discard the entire mixture and start over with a clean mason jar—and to release excess gas from the jar. If the carrots are not sour enough for your liking, let them ferment for a few more weeks.

4. Use the fermented carrots immediately or store them in the refrigerator for up to 2 months.

Strawberry & Basil Jam

The bright flavor of strawberries is brilliant when paired with soft herbs like basil. Fermentation adds another level of delicacy, which appeals to chefs like myself and my friend B. J., who is responsible for this preparation.

1 pint of fresh strawberries, picked over and hulled

1 bunch of fresh basil, chiffonade

Salt, as needed

1. Place a mixing bowl on a kitchen scale, tare it, and set the scale to measure grams.

2. Add the strawberries and basil to the bowl and weigh them. Add 2 percent of the mixture's weight in salt to the bowl. Stir to combine and place the mixture and any liquid in a vacuum bag in a single layer, or in a mason jar. If using a mason jar, place a fermentation weight on top of the mixture and make sure that the solids are completely submerged, adding water as needed.

3. Seal the container and place it in a dark, warm area for 2 days. Check the container every day to see if too much gas has built up. If it has, release the gas and reseal the container.

4. Strain the strawberry-and-basil mixture to remove the juices. Enjoy immediately or store in the refrigerator for up to 1 month. You can also can this jam, following the instructions on page 12.

Peaches & Honey

A recipe that showcases how fermentation is a great, accessible way for cooks of all levels to transform something as simple as a Sunday morning stack of pancakes.

1 lb. peaches, pits removed, finely diced

Salt, as needed

Honey, to taste

1. Place a mixing bowl on a kitchen scale, tare it, and set the scale to measure grams.

2. Add the peaches to the bowl and weigh them. Add 2 percent of the mixture's weight in salt to the bowl. Stir to combine and place the mixture and any liquid in a vacuum bag in a single layer, or in a mason jar. If using a mason jar, place a fermentation weight on top of the mixture and make sure that the solids are completely submerged.

3. Seal the container and place it in a dark, warm area until the flavor is to your liking, 2 to 5 days. Check the container every day to see if too much gas has built up. If it has, release the gas and reseal the container.

4. Strain the peaches, place them in a bowl, and add honey 1 teaspoon at a time until the mixture has the right balance of sweet and sour. Use immediately or store in the refrigerator.

Fruit Chutney

Meats hot off the grill will be the most desirable landing spot for this deeply flavored chutney, but it will also work well on a bowl of rice, brightening its neutral taste and color.

1 lb. mixed fresh fruit (such as apples, pears, and plums), peeled and chopped

Cloves from 1 head of garlic

1 teaspoon coarse sea salt

1 teaspoon sugar

1 cup apple cider vinegar

1. Place the fruit, garlic, salt, and sugar in a blender and puree until smooth.

2. Transfer the puree to a large jar and press down on it firmly with a wooden spoon to remove any air pockets.

3. Add the vinegar to the jar and stir to incorporate, making sure that the fruit puree is completely submerged.

4. Cover the jar with a tight-fitting lid or a cloth secured with a rubber band and place the jar in a warm, dark place until the flavor has developed to your liking, 7 to 10 days.

5. Use immediately or store the chutney in the refrigerator for up to 1 month. You can also can this chutney, following the instructions on page 12.

Fruit Chutney

See page 61

Spicy Sauerkraut

If you're partial to other accents like garlic, dill, or caraway in your sauerkraut, add them along with the red pepper flakes.

1 large head of green cabbage

2 tablespoons fine sea salt

1 teaspoon red pepper flakes

Water, as needed

1. Remove any wilted or damaged outer leaves from the cabbage. Cut the cabbage into quarters and remove the core. Slice the cabbage into thin shreds using a sharp knife or a mandoline.

2. Place the cabbage in a large bowl, add the salt and red pepper flakes, and massage the salt into the cabbage until the cabbage starts to release its liquid, about 5 minutes.

3. Transfer the cabbage and any liquid to a sterilized mason jar, pressing down firmly to remove any air pockets. The cabbage should be completely submerged in its own liquid. If it is not, add water as needed until the cabbage is submerged.

4. Seal the jar tightly and place the jar in a cool, dark place. Let it sit until the sauerkraut has a spicy, tangy flavor and a crunchy texture, 3 to 4 weeks. Check the jar every few days to make sure the cabbage is still fully submerged and release any excess gas. If the sauerkraut is not tangy enough after 4 weeks, let it ferment for a few more weeks.

5. Use the sauerkraut immediately or store it in the refrigerator for up to 2 months.

Lacto-Fermented Parsnips

For those who aren't super familiar with parsnips—think of them as nutty, even sweeter carrots. Fermentation will play up those two traits, and add a few others.

4 cups julienned parsnips

2 tablespoons fine sea salt

Water, as needed

1. Place the parsnips and salt in a bowl and massage the salt into the parsnips until they start to release their liquid, about 5 minutes.

2. Transfer the parsnips and their liquid to a large, sterilized mason jar, pressing down firmly to remove any air pockets. The parsnips should be completely submerged in their own liquid. If they are not, add water as needed until the parsnips are submerged.

3. Seal the jar tightly and place it in a cool, dark place until the flavor of the parsnips is slightly sour, and they have a slightly cloudy appearance, 3 to 4 weeks. Check the jar every few days day to make sure the carrots are fermenting properly—if you see any dark, moldy growth, discard the entire mixture and start over with a clean mason jar—and to release excess gas from the jar. If the parsnips are not sour enough for your liking, let them ferment for a few more weeks.

4. Use the fermented parsnips immediately or store them in the refrigerator for up to 2 months.

Fermented Beets

Beets are loaded with natural sugars, meaning the fermentation process has plenty to work its magic upon.

2 lbs. beets, peeled and julienned

¼ cup sea salt

1 tablespoon whole peppercorns

1 tablespoon dill seeds

1 teaspoon caraway seeds

1 teaspoon red pepper flakes (optional)

8 cups distilled water

2 cups white vinegar

1. Place the beets, salt, peppercorns, dill seeds, caraway seeds, and red pepper flakes (if using) in a large bowl and stir to combine.

2. Pack the beet mixture into a large, sterilized mason jar or crock, pressing down firmly to remove any air pockets.

3. Place the water and vinegar in a bowl and stir to combine. Pour the liquid over the beet mixture, making sure that it is fully submerged.

4. Seal the jar tightly and place it in a warm, dark place until the flavor of the beets is tangy and slightly spicy, and they have softened some, 2 to 3 weeks. Check the jar every few days day to make sure the beets are fermenting properly—if you see any dark, moldy growth, discard the entire mixture and start over with a clean mason jar—and to release excess gas from the jar. If the beets are not tangy enough for your liking, let them ferment for a few more days.

5. Use the beets immediately or store in the refrigerator for up to 2 months.

Fermented Cabbage

Fans of sauerkraut will be familiar with the flavor here, though the juniper berries and white vinegar add intriguing new levels above what you may expect.

2 lbs. green cabbage, finely shredded

¼ cup sea salt

1 tablespoon whole peppercorns

1 tablespoon juniper berries

1 teaspoon fennel seeds

1 teaspoon red pepper flakes (optional)

8 cups distilled water

2 cups white vinegar

1. Place the cabbage, salt, peppercorns, juniper berries, fennel seeds, and red pepper flakes (if using) in a large bowl and stir to combine.

2. Pack the cabbage mixture into a large, sterilized mason jar or crock, pressing down firmly to remove any air pockets.

3. Place the water and vinegar in a bowl and stir to combine. Pour the liquid over the cabbage mixture, making sure that it is fully submerged.

4. Seal the jar tightly and place it in a warm, dark place until the flavor of the cabbage is tangy and slightly spicy, and it has softened some, 2 to 3 weeks. Check the jar every few days day to make sure the cabbage is fermenting properly—if you see any dark, moldy growth, discard the entire mixture and start over with a clean mason jar—and to release excess gas from the jar. If the cabbage is not tangy enough for your liking, let it ferment for a few more days.

5. Use the cabbage immediately or store in the refrigerator for up to 2 months.

Yield: 8 Cups / **Active Time:** 20 Minutes / **Total Time:** 2 to 3 Weeks

Fermented Radishes

Ideal on a charcuterie board, where their bright and fresh taste will serve as wonderful counters to the other rich elements.

2 lbs. radishes, sliced thin

¼ cup sea salt

1½ tablespoons coriander seeds

1 teaspoon mustard seeds

2 teaspoons red pepper flakes (optional)

8 cups purified water

2 cups white vinegar

1. Place the radishes, salt, coriander seeds, mustard seeds, and red pepper flakes (if using) in a large bowl and stir to combine.

2. Pack the radish mixture into a large, sterilized mason jar or crock, pressing down firmly to remove any air pockets.

3. Place the water and vinegar in a bowl and stir to combine. Pour the liquid over the radish mixture, making sure that it is fully submerged.

4. Seal the jar tightly and place it in a warm, dark place until the flavor of the radishes is tangy and slightly spicy, and they have softened some, 2 to 3 weeks. Check the jar every few days day to make sure the radishes are fermenting properly—if you see any dark, moldy growth, discard the entire mixture and start over with a clean mason jar—and to release excess gas from the jar. If the radishes are not tangy enough for your liking, let them ferment for a few more days.

5. Use the radishes immediately or store them in the refrigerator for up to 2 months.

Fermented Radishes

See page 69

Fermented Eggplant

Think of this recipe as a jumping-off point for a new spin on your favorite mezze, whether it be baba ghanoush or hummus.

2 lbs. eggplant, sliced

¼ cup sea salt

1 tablespoon cumin seeds

1 tablespoon fennel seeds

1½ teaspoons mustard seeds

2 teaspoons red pepper flakes (optional)

8 cups purified water

2 cups white vinegar

1. Place the eggplant, salt, cumin seeds, fennel seeds, mustard seeds, and red pepper flakes (if using) in a large bowl and stir to combine.

2. Pack the eggplant mixture into a large, sterilized mason jar or crock, pressing down firmly to remove any air pockets.

3. Place the water and vinegar in a bowl and stir to combine. Pour the liquid over the eggplant mixture, making sure that it is fully submerged.

4. Seal the jar tightly and place it in a warm, dark place until the flavor of the eggplant is tangy and slightly spicy, and it has softened some, 2 to 3 weeks. Check the jar every few days day to make sure the eggplant is fermenting properly—if you see any dark, moldy growth, discard the entire mixture and start over with a clean mason jar—and to release excess gas from the jar. If the eggplant is not tangy enough for your liking, let it ferment for a few more days.

5. Use the eggplant immediately or store them in the refrigerator for up to 2 months.

Fermented Pineapple

A preparation made for the summer, it is as good on a bowl of ice cream as it is on a burger.

2 lbs. pineapple, peeled, cored, and diced

¼ cup sea salt

1 tablespoon whole cloves

2 teaspoons cinnamon

1 teaspoon ground ginger

2 teaspoons red pepper flakes (optional)

8 cups distilled water

2 cups honey

1. Place the pineapple, salt, cloves, cinnamon, ginger, and red pepper flakes (if using) in a large bowl and stir to combine.

2. Pack the pineapple mixture into a large, sterilized mason jar or crock, pressing down firmly to remove any air pockets.

3. Place the water and honey in a bowl and stir to combine. Pour the liquid over the pineapple mixture, making sure that it is fully submerged.

4. Seal the jar tightly and place it in a warm, dark place until the flavor of the pineapple is tangy, sweet, and slightly spicy, and it has softened some, 2 to 3 weeks. Check the jar every few days day to make sure the pineapple is fermenting properly—if you see any dark, moldy growth, discard the entire mixture and start over with a clean mason jar—and to release excess gas from the jar. If the pineapple is not tangy enough for your liking, let it ferment for a few more days.

5. Use the pineapple immediately or store it in the refrigerator for up to 2 months.

Fermented Pineapple

See page 73

Fermented Apples

As a longtime resident of New England, I'm always on the lookout for recipes that allow me to preserve the glory that is apple season.

2 lbs. apples, peeled, cored, and diced

¼ cup sea salt

1 tablespoon whole cloves

2 cinnamon sticks

1½ teaspoons freshly grated nutmeg

8 cups distilled water

2 cups honey

1. Place the apples, salt, cloves, cinnamon sticks, and nutmeg in a large bowl and stir to combine.

2. Pack the apple mixture into a large, sterilized mason jar or crock, pressing down firmly to remove any air pockets.

3. Place the water and honey in a bowl and stir to combine. Pour the liquid over the apple mixture, making sure that it is fully submerged.

4. Seal the jar tightly and place it in a warm, dark place until the flavor of the apples is tangy, sweet, and slightly spicy, and they have softened some, 2 to 3 weeks. Check the jar every few days day to make sure the apples are fermenting properly—if you see any dark, moldy growth, discard the entire mixture and start over with a clean mason jar—and to release excess gas from the jar. If the apples are not tangy enough for your liking, let them ferment for a few more days.

5. Use the apples immediately or store them in the refrigerator for up to 2 months.

Fermented Pears

A preparation capable of saving pears from their chronically underrated status, amplifying all of the subtle notes they contain.

2 lbs. pears, peeled, cored, and diced

¼ cup sea salt

1 tablespoon allspice berries

2 teaspoons juniper berries

1 teaspoon anise seeds

8 cups distilled water

2 cups honey

1. Place the pears, salt, allspice berries, juniper berries, and anise seeds in a large bowl and stir to combine.

2. Pack the pear mixture into a large, sterilized mason jar or crock, pressing down firmly to remove any air pockets.

3. Place the water and honey in a bowl and stir to combine. Pour the liquid over the pear mixture, making sure that it is fully submerged.

4. Seal the jar tightly and place it in a warm, dark place until the flavor of the pears is tangy, sweet, and slightly spicy, and they have softened some, 2 to 3 weeks. Check the jar every few days day to make sure the pears are fermenting properly—if you see any dark, moldy growth, discard the entire mixture and start over with a clean mason jar—and to release excess gas from the jar. If the pears are not tangy enough for your liking, let them ferment for a few more days.

5. Use the pears immediately or store them in the refrigerator for up to 2 months.

Fermented Berries

You can leave these berries as is after fermenting, or cook them down and use them as jam.

2 lbs. fresh berries (raspberries, blueberries, blackberries, etc.)

¼ cup sea salt

1 tablespoon whole black peppercorns

1 teaspoon cinnamon

8 cups distilled water

2 cups honey

1. In a large bowl, mix together the mixed berries, salt, peppercorns, and cinnamon.

2. Pack the berry mixture into a large, sterilized mason jar or crock, pressing down firmly to remove any air pockets.

3. Place the water and honey in a bowl and stir to combine. Pour the liquid over the berry mixture, making sure that it is fully submerged.

4. Seal the jar tightly and place it in a warm, dark place until the flavor of the berries is tangy, sweet, and slightly spicy, and they have softened some, 2 to 3 weeks. Check the jar every few days day to make sure the berries are fermenting properly—if you see any dark, moldy growth, discard the entire mixture and start over with a clean mason jar—and to release excess gas from the jar. If the berries are not tangy enough for your liking, let them ferment for a few more days.

5. Use the berries immediately or store them in the refrigerator for up to 2 months.

Rice & Legumes

As rice is a staple food in Asia, people have continually sought ways to make use of it. One of the best results of this experimentation is dosa, a South Indian delicacy that resides somewhere between pita bread and Ethiopian injera. Appearing in numerous forms, dosa can function as a wrap, a flatbread, or an intriguing inclusion on a charcuterie board, and while it is a preparation that takes some time to get a handle on, those who persevere will have an entire new world opened up.

Lentils and beans are other staples that have been fermented to produce dishes that seem completely removed from the ingredients that form their basis—particularly idli, a soft and spongy cake made from rice and lentils that can become a go-to no matter the time of day.

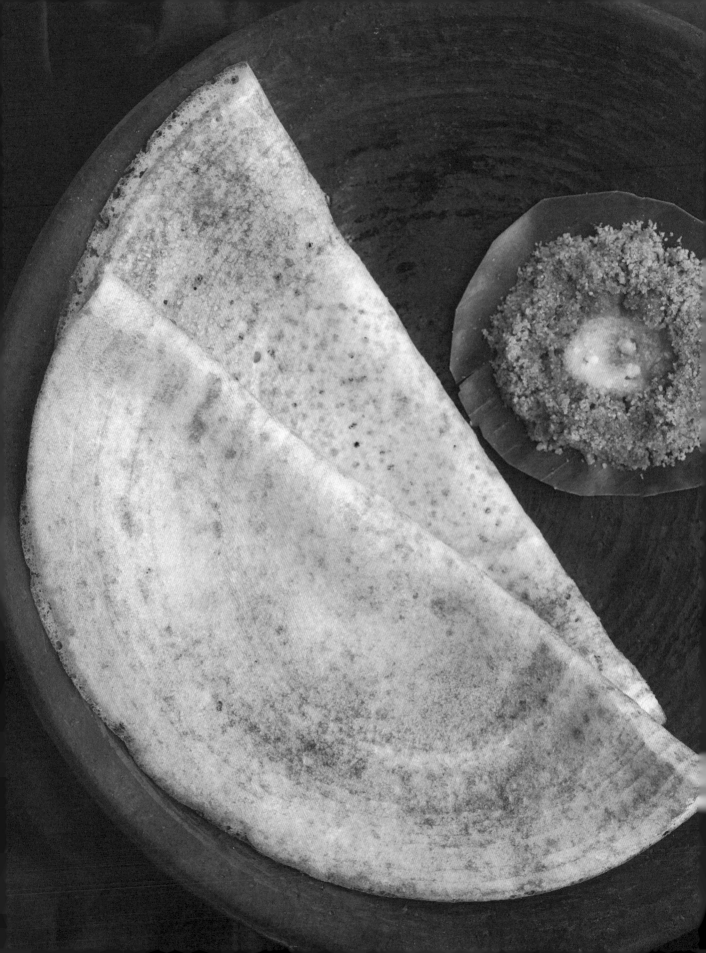

Dosa

Popular across India, with roots in Southern India, a trip to the nearest South Asian grocery store will help quite a bit with acquiring the components of this recipe. Once you do, be aware that dosa take a lot of practice to get correct, and that they are well worth that effort.

2 cups rice (idli is recommended)

½ cup black split lentils

2 teaspoons fenugreek seeds

¼ cup flat rice (poha)

1 teaspoon kosher salt

1. Place the rice in a bowl, cover it with water, and let it soak at room temperature for 8 hours.

2. Place the lentils and fenugreek seeds in a separate bowl, cover the mixture with water, and let it soak at room temperature for 4 hours. Transfer the mixture to the refrigerator and chill it for 4 hours.

3. Drain the lentil mixture, place it in a blender, and puree until it is smooth. Drain the soaked rice and add it to the blender along with the flat rice and salt. Puree until the mixture is smooth.

4. Transfer the mixture to a large mixing bowl and work the mixture with clean hands. The heat from your hands will begin to activate the natural fermentation process.

5. Cover the bowl and either place it in the oven with the light on, or in an incubator set to 80°F. Let the batter ferment until it becomes fluffy and doubles in size, 12 to 16 hours. This fermentation period will make the batter slightly sour and delicious.

6. To make the dosa, warm a skillet over medium-high heat. Place a ladleful of the batter in the pan and use the bottom of the ladle to spread it out into a thin circle. Cook until the dosa is crispy, fold it in half, and transfer it to a plate. Repeat with the remaining batter. If you are not making dosa right away, the batter will keep in the refrigerator, covered, for up to 1 week.

Yield: 10 Servings / **Active Time:** 20 Minutes / **Total Time:** 24 Hours

Set Dosa

Set dosa, also known as sponge dosa, are popular in the Indian states of Bangalore and Karnataka, where they are often topped with a coconut chutney.

2 cups rice (idli is recommended)

½ cup black lentils

2 teaspoons fenugreek seeds

1 cup flat rice (poha)

1 teaspoon kosher salt

1. Working with one item at a time, rinse the rice and lentils under cold water until the water is clear.

2. Place the rice in a bowl, cover it with cold water, and let it soak at room temperature for 8 hours.

3. Place the lentils and fenugreek seeds in a separate bowl, cover the mixture with water, and let it soak at room temperature for 4 hours. Transfer the mixture to the refrigerator and chill it for 4 hours.

4. Drain the lentil mixture, place it in a blender, and puree until it is smooth. Drain the soaked rice and add it to the blender along with the flat rice and salt. Puree until the mixture is smooth.

5. Transfer the mixture to a large mixing bowl and work the mixture with clean hands. The heat from your hands will begin to activate the natural fermentation process.

6. Cover the bowl and either place it in the oven with the light on, or in an incubator set to 80°F. Let the batter ferment until it becomes fluffy and doubles in size, 12 to 16 hours. This fermentation period will make the batter slightly sour and delicious.

7. To make the dosa, warm a skillet over medium-high heat. Place a ladleful of the batter in the pan and use the bottom of the ladle to spread it out slightly, leaving it as a thick circle. Cook the dosa for 3 minutes, cover the pan, and cook until the top is set, 2 to 3 minutes. Transfer the dosa to a plate and repeat with the remaining batter. If you are not making dosa right away, the batter will keep in the refrigerator, covered, for up to 1 week.

Uttapam

What to do with leftover dosa batter? Make uttapam, a pancake-like delicacy that can support a variety of toppings. If you don't have any leftover dosa batter, you can use the preparation for Set Dosa (see page 84) and store it in the refrigerator for 1 week after the 12- to 16-hour fermentation period.

Leftover dosa batter

1. Place the dosa batter in the refrigerator, cover it, and let it sit for 1 week. The batter will get even more sour as it rests, which is the key to uttapam.

2. To make the uttapam, warm a large skillet over medium-high heat. Place a heaping ladleful of the batter in the center of the pan and cook until the bottom is golden brown, 4 to 6 minutes. Reduce the heat to medium-low, cover the pan, and cook the uttapam until it is cooked through, 3 to 5 minutes. Transfer the uttapam to a plate and repeat with the remaining batter.

Ragi Dosa

Rich with iron and fiber and carrying an addictive nutty flavor, red millet, or finger millet, forms the foundation of this delicious dosa.

½ cup red millet

½ cup rice (idli is recommended)

½ cup black lentils

1 teaspoon fenugreek seeds

1 teaspoon kosher salt

1. Rinse the red millet and rice under cold water until the water is clear.

2. Place the millet and rice in a bowl, cover it with cold water, and let it soak at room temperature for 8 hours.

3. Place the lentils and fenugreek seeds in a separate bowl, cover the mixture with water, and let it soak at room temperature for 4 hours. Transfer the mixture to the refrigerator and chill it for 4 hours.

4. Drain the lentil mixture, place it in a blender, and puree until it is smooth. Drain the soaked rice and millet and add it to the blender along with the salt. Puree until the mixture is smooth.

5. Transfer the mixture to a large mixing bowl and work the mixture with clean hands. The heat from your hands will begin to activate the natural fermentation process.

6. Cover the bowl and either place it in the oven with the light on, or in an incubator set to 80°F. Let the batter ferment until it becomes fluffy and doubles in size, 10 to 12 hours. This fermentation period will make the batter slightly sour and delicious.

7. To make the dosa, warm a skillet over medium-high heat. Place a ladleful of the batter in the pan and use the bottom of the ladle to spread it out into a thin circle. Cook until the dosa is crispy, fold it in half, and transfer it to a plate. Repeat with the remaining batter. If you are not making dosa right away, the batter will keep in the refrigerator, covered, for up to 1 week.

Ragi Dosa

See page 87

Fermented Saffron Rice

An irresistible recipe, with the saffron adding a rich, fragrant aroma that draws you into the tangy, sour taste.

1 cup long-grain white rice

¼ teaspoon saffron threads

¼ teaspoon coarse sea salt

1½ cups filtered water

1. Rinse the rice under cold, running water until the water runs clear.

2. Place the rice in a small saucepan and add the saffron, salt, and water. Bring the mixture to a boil over medium-high heat, reduce the heat to low, and cover the pan. Simmer the rice until it has absorbed the water and is tender, 18 to 20 minutes.

3. Transfer the rice to a large mason jar and press down on it with a wooden spoon to remove any air pockets.

4. Cover the jar with a tight-fitting lid or a cloth secured with a rubber band and place the jar in a warm, dark place until the flavor has developed to your liking, 3 to 5 days.

5. Fluff the rice with a fork and enjoy, or store it in the refrigerator.

Appe

Traditionally, this high-protein, low-fat South Indian dish would be prepared in a special pan featuring shallow, circular molds that the batter is spooned into.

1 cup black lentils

1 cup semolina

1 cup water

1 teaspoon coarse sea salt

1 teaspoon baking soda

2 tablespoons avocado oil

1. Place all of the ingredients, except for the avocado oil, in a mixing bowl and stir until the mixture comes together as a smooth batter.

2. Pour the mixture into a large mason jar and cover the jar with a tight-fitting lid or a cloth secured with a rubber band. Place the jar in a warm, dark place for 8 to 12 hours.

3. Place some of the avocado oil in a large skillet and warm it over medium heat. Drop spoonfuls of the batter into the pan, making sure to leave enough space between each one. Cook until the bottoms are golden brown.

4. Turn the appe over and cook until the other side is golden brown. Remove the cooked appe from the pan and enjoy once all of the batter has been cooked, adding the remaining avocado oil as needed.

Idli

Idli's soft and spongy texture is a result of allowing the batter to ferment for a while. Once it does, it can work at breakfast, lunch, dinner, or as a snack.

2 cups uncooked parboiled rice

1 cup black lentils

1 teaspoon fenugreek seeds

1 teaspoon coarse sea salt

1. Rinse the rice and lentils under cold water until the water is clear.

2. Place the rice and lentils in a bowl, cover the mixture with cold water, and let it soak at room temperature for 6 hours.

3. Drain the mixture, place it in a blender, and add the fenugreek seeds and salt. Puree until the mixture is smooth.

4. Pour the puree into a large mason jar and cover the jar with a tight-fitting lid or a cloth secured with a rubber band. Place the jar in a warm, dark place for 8 to 12 hours.

5. Coat the wells of an idli pan with nonstick cooking spray and fill them with the batter. Bring a few inches of water to a simmer and set a steaming basket over the simmering water. Place the idli pan in the basket and steam the idli until they are cooked through.

6. Remove the idli from the pan and enjoy. If you are not making idli right away, the batter will keep in the refrigerator, covered, for a few days.

Idli

See page 93

Mor Kuzhambhu

Split pigeon peas, coconut milk, and bold seasonings combine to make this heady, creamy South Indian favorite.

1 cup split pigeon peas

1 cup water

1 cup coconut milk

1 cup buttermilk

1 teaspoon ghee

1 teaspoon mustard seeds

1 teaspoon cumin seeds

1 teaspoon split black lentils

1 teaspoon split chickpeas

1 green chile pepper, stem and seeds removed, minced

Leaves from 1 sprig of fresh curry

1 teaspoon kosher salt

1. Place the split pigeon peas in a large bowl, cover them with water, and let them soak for 6 hours.

2. Drain the split pigeon peas and place them in a blender. Add the water, coconut milk, and buttermilk and puree until the mixture is smooth and creamy.

3. Pour the mixture into a large mason jar and cover the jar with a tight-fitting lid or a cloth secured with a rubber band. Place the jar in a warm, dark place for 8 to 12 hours.

4. Transfer the mixture to the refrigerator and let it sit until it is chilled.

5. Place the ghee in a large saucepan and warm it over medium heat. Add the mustard seeds, cumin seeds, split black lentils, and split chickpeas and cook until the seeds start to pop and the split chickpeas turn golden brown, 1 to 2 minutes.

6. Stir in the chile and curry leaves and cook for 1 to 2 minutes.

7. Add the mor kuzhambu and salt, reduce the heat to medium-low, and cook, stirring occasionally, for 10 minutes. Serve immediately.

Dhokla

The key to achieving a light, spongy texture in dhokla is the reaction between the eno fruit salt and the citric acid in the lemon juice, which creates enough carbon dioxide to leaven the batter.

1 cup dried/uncooked split chickpeas

1 cup water

1 teaspoon salt

1 teaspoon sugar

1 teaspoon fresh lemon juice

1 teaspoon eno fruit salt

1. Place the split chickpeas in a large bowl, cover them with water, and let them soak for 6 hours.

2. Drain the chickpeas and place them in a blender. Add the water, salt, sugar, and lemon juice and puree until the mixture is smooth and creamy.

3. Pour the mixture into a large mason jar and cover the jar with a tight-fitting lid or a cloth secured with a rubber band. Place the jar in a warm, dark place for 8 to 12 hours.

4. Transfer the batter to the refrigerator and let it sit until it is chilled.

5. Stir the eno fruit salt into the chilled batter. Coat a dhokla stand or a round 9-inch cake pan with nonstick cooking spray. Bring a few inches of water to a simmer and place a steaming basket over the simmering water.

6. Pour the dhokla into the chosen pan and place it in the steaming basket. Steam the dhokla until it is cooked through and a toothpick inserted into the center comes out clean, 15 to 20 minutes. Serve immediately. If you are not making dhokla immediately, the batter will keep in the refrigerator for several days.

Dhokla

See page 97

Natto

This preparation is something of an acquired taste, due to its pungent odor and slippery texture, but it pays off any investment with a unique taste and a whole host of vitamins.

1 cup dried soybeans

1 teaspoon natto spores
(also called natto-kin)

1. Place the soybeans in a large bowl and cover them with water. Soak them for at least 8 hours or overnight.

2. Drain the soybeans and place them in a rice cooker. Alternatively, you can place them in a steaming basket, bring a few inches of water to a simmer, and place the steaming basket over the water. Steam the soybeans until they are soft and easily mashed, about 1 hour.

3. Remove the soybeans from the rice cooker or steaming basket and let them cool until they are at least 77°F.

4. Place the soybeans in a clean, dry bowl, add the natto spores, and stir until they are evenly distributed.

5. Place the mixture in a jar, seal it, and place it in an incubator or a naturally warm place that is at least 77°F. Let the mixture sit for 24 to 48 hours.

6. When the natto is ready, it will have a slimy texture and a strong, pungent aroma. If the natto is not slimy or pungent enough, you can leave it to ferment for a few more hours or days.

7. Use immediately or store the natto in the refrigerator for up to 1 week.

Masoor Dal Tofu

Red lentils, sometimes referred to as masoor dal, are a tiny, orange-colored legume that are frequently used in Middle Eastern and Indian cooking. When cooked, they have has a mildly nutty flavor and a smooth, creamy texture.

¾ cup split red lentils

1½ cups boiling water

1½ cups room-temperature water

1 tablespoon nutritional yeast

1 teaspoon kosher salt

1. Place the lentils in a bowl, cover them with the boiling water, and let them soak for 15 minutes.

2. Drain the lentils, place them in a blender, and puree until smooth.

3. Place the lentil puree in a saucepan, add the remaining ingredients, and cook the mixture over medium heat, whisking continually, until it thickens, 10 to 15 minutes.

4. Once thickened, transfer the mixture to a pan or container, cover it, and let the tofu cool for 8 hours.

5. Use the tofu immediately or store in the refrigerator, where it will keep for a few days.

Tempeh

This fermented soybean cake is a reliable protein source around the world, particularly in Indonesia, where it originated. Tempeh starter can be purchased at health-food stores, or online.

1 lb. dried whole soybeans   2 tablespoons white vinegar   1 teaspoon tempeh starter

1. Place the soybeans in a large bowl and cover them by 3 inches with water. Soak for at least 12 hours or overnight.

2. Remove the hulls from the beans, using your hands or a potato masher to press against the beans until they split in half. This may take 10 to 20 minutes. Stir the water occasionally to help the hulls float to the surface, remove them as they do, and discard.

3. Drain the hulled beans, place them in a large saucepan, and cover them with water. Bring to a boil, skimming to remove any foam or hulls that rise to the surface. Reduce the heat, partially cover the pan, and simmer the beans until they are tender but before they become mushy, about 45 minutes.

4. While the beans are cooking, prepare two resealable bags, using a skewer to prick holes in them at 1-inch intervals. Line two baking sheets with paper towels. Drain the beans and spread them out on the baking sheets. Pat them dry and let them cool to just below body temperature.

5. Place the beans in a clean, dry bowl, add the vinegar, and stir to combine. This will lower the pH and prevent the growth of unwanted bacteria. Add the tempeh starter and stir for about 1 minute to ensure that it is evenly distributed. Divide the beans between the two bags and seal them. Flatten the beans out so that they sit in even layers.

6. Set the temperature in an incubator somewhere between 85°F and 90°F. Place the bags in the incubator and let them sit for 24 to 48 hours, periodically checking the temperature inside the incubator to make sure it remains in the correct range. After 12 to 24 hours, you should start to see white mycelium growing on the beans. When you see this, you may need to lower the temperature, as the beans will start generating their own heat as the mold grows. Depending on the conditions, the tempeh may take up to 48 hours total. The mycelium will continue to thicken, forming a white layer around the beans and binding them into a dense, firm cake. The tempeh is done when the entire surface is covered with dense, white mycelium (some black or gray spots are normal) and the beans are bound together firmly as a cake. You may want to slice off a small piece to make sure the cake is firm all the way through. The tempeh should have a pleasantly nutty and mushroomy aroma, and may also have a slight tinge of ammonia.

7. Remove the bags from the incubator and let the tempeh cool to room temperature. Transfer the tempeh cakes to airtight bags or containers and store in the refrigerator for up to 1 week.

Tempeh

See page 103

Yogurt

People who frequent the grocery store and routinely pass by an entire aisle of yogurt available at very affordable prices might look at this chapter and wonder why anyone would bother to make their own at home. Well, it turns out that much of that yogurt at the store isn't yogurt per se—almost all of the helpful probiotics and nutrients that have been processed out, meaning that the enormous health benefits that have made yogurt a beloved staple in cultures across the globe are absent.

Making yogurt at home, while definitely a commitment, ensures that all of the benefits that you automatically associate with it are present. Whether you're looking to improve your gut health or get protein in a more digestible form than you can elsewhere, this chapter is a master class in how to make bacteria work for, rather than against, you.

Homemade Yogurt

My go-to recipe for yogurt—easy for the beginner, and satisfying for the expert.

8 cups whole milk

½ cup store-bought yogurt with active cultures (organic yogurt preferred)

1. Place the milk in a large saucepan and warm it, stirring frequently, until it is approximately 200°F. Make sure that the milk does not come to a boil, as it will change the protein structure.

2. Remove the milk from heat and let it cool to 112°F to 115°F, stirring occasionally to prevent a skin from forming.

3. Whisk the milk. Add the store-bought yogurt and continue to whisk. When the temperature is 110°F, place the mixture in an insulated thermos, maintaining a temperature of 110°F.

4. After 4 hours, the yogurt will be set. If you prefer a thicker yogurt, keep it in the thermos until the desired consistency has been achieved. Transfer the yogurt to a container, cover it, and let the yogurt cool completely before serving or storing in the refrigerator.

Yogurt with Whey Fermented Berries

In summertime, we are blessed with a variety of berries. One of the challenges is to find innovative ways to use them, a charge fermentation is always ready to meet. Whey is a byproduct of dairy, the watery mixture you see on top of yogurt. When you make cheese, whey is what's left over and it contains a lot of beneficial bacteria that positively affect the flavor and nutritional value of whatever it comes in contact with.

4 cups Homemade Yogurt (see page 108), plus more for serving

2 pints of your preferred berries

1. Line a sieve with cheesecloth and place it over a large bowl. Pour the yogurt into the sieve and press down to remove as much liquid as possible. You should have approximately 1 cup of liquid, which is the whey you will use to ferment the berries. Set the whey and the strained yogurt aside.

2. Place the berries in a large, sterilized mason jar. Cover them with the whey, making sure they are completely submerged, and then cover the jar with a piece of cloth and secure with a rubber band. Let the jar sit in a cool, dark place for 5 to 7 days. You will see bubbles form and rise to the top as the mixture ferments.

3. When ready to use, strain the mixture and serve the fermented berries over yogurt. Store any leftover berries in the refrigerator for up to 1 week.

Greek Yogurt

By eliminating the whey from conventional yogurt, Greek yogurt becomes thicker and creamier, while remaining a fantastic source of calcium, protein, and probiotics.

4 cups milk

2 tablespoons plain Greek yogurt

1. Place the milk in a medium saucepan and warm it over medium heat until it is about 185°F to 190°F. The milk should be steaming and have a thin skin on top.

2. Remove the pan from heat and let the milk cool until it reaches about 110°F to 115°F.

3. Place the milk in a large bowl, add the yogurt, and whisk to combine.

4. Pour the mixture into a large mason jar and cover the jar with a tight-fitting lid or a cloth secured with a rubber band. Place the jar in a warm, dark place for 8 to 12 hours.

5. Line a colander with cheesecloth and pour the yogurt into it. Let the yogurt drain for 1 hour.

6. Use the yogurt immediately or store it in the refrigerator, where it will keep for a few days.

Labneh

Think of this as Greek yogurt allowed to drain for an exceptionally long time, so that it becomes closer to cheese in its consistency. This is wonderful spread over some pita bread or with crudités, and feel to top it with olive oil and your favorite seasonings.

1 cup Greek Yogurt
(see page 112)

1 teaspoon kosher salt

1. Place the yogurt in a mixing bowl, add the salt, and stir to combine.

2. Place a piece of cheesecloth over a bowl and scoop the yogurt into the cheesecloth. Fold up the cheesecloth and secure it with a string or rubber band.

3. Suspend the cheesecloth over the bowl so that it hangs down but does not touch the bottom of the bowl. Cover the bowl with plastic wrap and chill it in the refrigerator overnight.

4. The next morning, discard the liquid in the bowl. Remove the labneh from the cheesecloth and use immediately or store it in the refrigerator.

Blueberry Labneh

The blueberries will acquire a bit more sourness as they sit, but their natural sweetness is what shines here.

1 cup fresh blueberries

1 cup Greek Yogurt
(see page 112)

1 teaspoon kosher salt

1. Place the blueberries in a bowl and mash them.

2. Place the yogurt in a mixing bowl, add the blueberries and salt, and stir to combine.

3. Place a piece of cheesecloth over a bowl and scoop the yogurt mixture into the cheesecloth. Fold up the cheesecloth and secure it with a string or rubber band.

4. Suspend the cheesecloth over the bowl so that it hangs down but does not touch the bottom of the bowl. Cover the bowl with plastic wrap and chill it in the refrigerator overnight.

5. The next morning, discard the liquid in the bowl. Remove the labneh from the cheesecloth and use immediately or store it in the refrigerator.

Strawberry Labneh

If you're going to use this as a desserty dip, consider topping it with some lemon zest or graham cracker crumbs.

1 cup fresh strawberries, hulled and chopped

1 cup Greek Yogurt (see page 112)

1 teaspoon kosher salt

1. Place the strawberries in a bowl and mash them.

2. Place the yogurt in a mixing bowl, add the strawberries and salt, and stir to combine.

3. Place a piece of cheesecloth over a bowl and scoop the yogurt mixture into the cheesecloth. Fold up the cheesecloth and secure it with a string or rubber band.

4. Suspend the cheesecloth over the bowl so that it hangs down but does not touch the bottom of the bowl. Cover the bowl with plastic wrap and chill it in the refrigerator overnight.

5. The next morning, discard the liquid in the bowl. Remove the labneh from the cheesecloth and use immediately or store it in the refrigerator.

Strawberry Labneh

See page 117

Dahi

Dahi is a fermented dairy product that is created by adding active cultures to milk and letting it ferment for a while. The end product, which is often referred to as "yogurt" or "curd," is thick, creamy, and protein-rich. Enjoy it as is, or use it in place of mayonnaise or sour cream.

4 cups milk

2 tablespoons plain yogurt

1. Place the milk in a medium saucepan and warm it over medium heat until it is about 185°F to 190°F. The milk should be steaming and have a thin skin on top.

2. Remove the pan from heat and let the milk cool until it reaches about 110°F to 115°F.

3. Place the milk in a large bowl, add the yogurt, and whisk to combine.

4. Pour the mixture into a large mason jar and cover the jar with a tight-fitting lid or a cloth secured with a rubber band. Place the jar in a warm, dark place for 8 to 12 hours.

5. Use the dahi immediately or store it in the refrigerator, where it will keep for a few days.

Rava Idli

Compared to the conventional version of idli (see page 93), rava idli has a softer and more delicate texture thanks to the semolina, while the yogurt and spices give the dish flavor and depth.

1 cup semolina

1 cup plain yogurt

1 cup water

1 teaspoon coarse sea salt

1 teaspoon baking soda

1. Place all of the ingredients in a mixing bowl and stir until the mixture comes together as a smooth batter.

2. Pour the mixture into a large mason jar and cover the jar with a tight-fitting lid or a cloth secured with a rubber band. Place the jar in a warm, dark place for 8 to 12 hours.

3. Coat the wells of an idli pan with nonstick cooking spray and fill them with the batter. Bring a few inches of water to a simmer and set a steaming basket over the simmering water. Place the idli pan in the basket and steam the idli until they are cooked through.

4. Remove the idli from the pan and enjoy. If you are not making idli right away, the batter will keep in the refrigerator, covered, for a few days.

Beverages

Of course, beer, wine, and Champagne are the clear cream of the crop when it comes to fermented beverages. And while their production have all risen to a level of craft that is hard to reach at home, that does not mean that the fermentation enthusiast is out of luck if they want to incorporate their passion into what they drink.

As those who frequent a farmers market, craft coffee purveyor, or co-operative grocery store have no doubt noticed, kombucha has stormed onto the scene, with offerings from numerous companies now widely available. That sudden surge of availability is due to kombucha's ability to work with numerous fruits and flavors, countering their sweetness with a unique tartness, and adding the beneficial bacteria that everyone is suddenly buzzing about.

One thing to keep in mind: the fermentation process in preparations like kombucha and tepache does produce alcohol in small amounts, so if you're focused on sobriety, you might want to steer clear of these recipes and turn to the other preparations in this book for a fermentation fix.

Kombucha

The base of every kombucha recipe you can think of. If you choose to retain the SCOBY (symbiotic culture of bacteria and yeast) for future batches of kombucha, keep in mind that you should peel off the layers as it thickens and give them to friends who are interested in following your lead and brewing kombucha at home.

16 cups water

4 bags of tea

1 cup sugar

¼ cup kombucha from a previous batch

1. Place the water in a large saucepan and bring it to a gentle simmer. Add the tea bags and sugar and stir until the sugar has dissolved and the tea has steeped. Remove the pan from heat, remove the tea bags, and let the tea cool to room temperature.

2. Place the tea in a large container, add the kombucha, and cover the container with a piece of cheesecloth. Secure the cheesecloth with a rubber band, place the container in a warm, dark place, and let it ferment until the flavor has developed to your liking, 3 to 7 days.

3. Strain the kombucha to remove the SCOBY and reserve ¼ cup for the next batch.

4. Pour the kombucha into large, sterilized mason jars. Seal them tight and place them in a warm, dark place until the kombucha has the desired level of carbonation, about 3 days.

5. Test a jar by slowly and carefully releasing the top—there should be an audible noise signifying carbonation.

6. Place the jars in the refrigerator and let them cool completely before enjoying. Store in the refrigerator, as kombucha will continue to ferment rapidly at room temperature.

Blackberry & Lime Kombucha

These first four kombucha recipes are all from my friend, B. J. Beisler, and this sweet-and-sour brew is his favorite of the bunch.

16 cups water

4 bags of tea

1 cup sugar

¼ cup kombucha from a previous batch

2 pints of fresh blackberries

Zest of 2 limes

1. Place the water in a large saucepan and bring it to a gentle simmer. Add the tea bags and sugar and stir until the sugar has dissolved and the tea has steeped. Remove the pan from heat, remove the tea bags, and let the tea cool to room temperature.

2. Place the tea in a large container, add the kombucha, and cover the container with a piece of cheesecloth. Secure the cheesecloth with a rubber band, place the container in a warm, dark place, and let it ferment until the flavor has developed to your liking, 3 to 7 days.

3. Strain the kombucha to remove the SCOBY and reserve ¼ cup for the next batch.

4. Place the blackberries and lime zest in a blender and puree until smooth. Strain the puree and stir it into the kombucha.

5. Pour the kombucha into large, sterilized mason jars. Seal them tight and place them in a warm, dark place until the kombucha has the desired level of carbonation, about 3 days.

6. Test 1 jar by slowly and carefully releasing the top—there should be an audible noise signifying carbonation.

7. Place the jars in the refrigerator and let them cool completely before enjoying. Store in the refrigerator, as kombucha will continue to ferment rapidly at room temperature.

Maple Kombucha

In New England, maple is religion, and this kombucha pays proper homage.

16 cups water

4 bags of tea

1 cup sugar

¼ cup kombucha from a previous batch

2 cups high-quality maple syrup

1. Place the water in a large saucepan and bring it to a gentle simmer. Add the tea bags and sugar and stir until the sugar has dissolved and the tea has steeped. Remove the pan from heat, remove the tea bags, and let the tea cool to room temperature.

2. Place the tea in a large container, add the kombucha, and cover the container with a piece of cheesecloth. Secure the cheesecloth with a rubber band, place the container in a warm, dark place, and let it ferment until the flavor has developed to your liking, 3 to 7 days.

3. Strain the kombucha to remove the SCOBY and reserve ¼ cup for the next batch.

4. Stir the maple syrup into the kombucha and pour the kombucha into large, sterilized mason jars. Seal them tight and place them in a warm, dark place until the kombucha has the desired level of carbonation, about 3 days.

5. Test 1 jar by slowly and carefully releasing the top—there should be an audible noise signifying carbonation.

6. Place the jars in the refrigerator and let them cool completely before enjoying. Store in the refrigerator, as kombucha will continue to ferment rapidly at room temperature.

Strawberry & Lemon Kombucha

Nothing screams summer more than strawberry and lemon.

16 cups water

4 bags of tea

1 cup sugar

¼ cup kombucha from a previous batch

2 pints of fresh strawberries, hulled

Zest of 2 lemons

1. Place the water in a large saucepan and bring it to a gentle simmer. Add the tea bags and sugar and stir until the sugar has dissolved and the tea has steeped. Remove the pan from heat, remove the tea bags, and let the tea cool to room temperature.

2. Place the tea in a large container, add the kombucha, and cover the container with a piece of cheesecloth. Secure the cheesecloth with a rubber band, place the container in a warm, dark place, and let it ferment until the flavor has developed to your liking, 3 to 7 days.

3. Strain the kombucha to remove the SCOBY and reserve ¼ cup for the next batch.

4. Place the strawberries and lemon zest in a blender and puree until smooth. Strain the puree and stir it into the kombucha.

5. Pour the kombucha into large, sterilized mason jars. Seal them tight and place them in a warm, dark place until the kombucha has the desired level of carbonation, about 3 days.

6. Test 1 jar by slowly and carefully releasing the top—there should be an audible noise signifying carbonation.

7. Place the jars in the refrigerator and let them cool completely before enjoying. Store in the refrigerator, as kombucha will continue to ferment rapidly at room temperature.

Strawberry &
Lemon Kombucha

See page 131

Strawberry Kombucha

Strawberry picking is a great way to spend a late-spring day, and this bright kombucha is a wonderful way to use up some of your haul.

16 cups water

1 cup white sugar

8 bags of black or green tea

SCOBY (optional)

2 cups kombucha from a previous batch

1 cup mashed strawberries

1. Place the water in a stockpot and bring it to a boil. Add the sugar and tea, remove the pan from heat, and let the mixture steep for 10 minutes. Remove the bags of tea, discard them, and let the mixture cool to room temperature.

2. Place the SCOBY (if using), kombucha, and cooled tea in a large container or fermenting vessel. Add the strawberries and stir until thoroughly combined.

3. Cover the container with a cloth and secure it with a rubber band. Place the jar in a warm, dark place and let it ferment until the flavor is fruity and slightly tangy and it has a slightly cloudy appearance, 3 to 4 weeks. Check the container every few days to make sure the kombucha is fermenting properly. If the kombucha is not tangy enough for your liking, you can leave it to ferment for a few more weeks.

4. Strain the kombucha through cheesecloth and serve it over ice or store it in the refrigerator.

Yield: 16 Cups / **Active Time:** 20 Minutes / **Total Time:** 3 to 4 Weeks

Blueberry Kombucha

A perfect kombucha to sip in the shade during the dog days of summer.

16 cups water

1 cup white sugar

8 bags of black or green tea

SCOBY (optional)

2 cups kombucha from a previous batch

1 cup mashed blueberries

1. Place the water in a stockpot and bring it to a boil. Add the sugar and tea, remove the pan from heat, and let the mixture steep for 10 minutes. Remove the bags of tea, discard them, and let the mixture cool to room temperature.

2. Place the SCOBY (if using), kombucha, and cooled tea in a large container or fermenting vessel. Add the blueberries and stir until thoroughly combined.

3. Cover the container with a cloth and secure it with a rubber band. Place the jar in a warm, dark place and let it ferment until the flavor is fruity and slightly tangy and it has a slightly cloudy appearance, 3 to 4 weeks. Check the container every few days to make sure the kombucha is fermenting properly. If the kombucha is not tangy enough for your liking, you can leave it to ferment for a few more weeks.

4. Strain the kombucha through cheesecloth and serve it over ice or store it in the refrigerator.

Mango Kombucha

The tropical, slightly piney flavor of mango is wonderful when set off by the subtle sour taste cultivated during fermentation.

16 cups water

1 cup white sugar

8 bags of black or green tea

1 cup SCOBY (optional)

2 cups kombucha from a previous batch

1 cup mashed mango

1. Place the water in a stockpot and bring it to a boil. Add the sugar and tea, remove the pan from heat, and let the mixture steep for 10 minutes. Remove the bags of tea, discard them, and let the mixture cool to room temperature.

2. Place the SCOBY (if using), kombucha, and cooled tea in a large container or fermenting vessel. Add the mango and stir until thoroughly combined.

3. Cover the container with a cloth and secure it with a rubber band. Place the container in a warm, dark place and let it ferment until the flavor is fruity and slightly tangy and it has a slightly cloudy appearance, 3 to 4 weeks. Check the container every few days to make sure the kombucha is fermenting properly. If the kombucha is not tangy enough for your liking, you can leave it to ferment for a few more weeks.

4. Strain the kombucha through cheesecloth and serve it over ice or store it in the refrigerator.

Tepache

This fermented beverage uses the whole pineapple to create a refreshing and salubrious tonic. Tepache can be made with other fruits if pineapple is not available.

32 cups water

4 oz. piloncillo

1 large cinnamon stick

3 whole cloves

1 pineapple

1. Place half of the water, the piloncillo, cinnamon, and cloves in a large saucepan and warm over medium heat, stirring to dissolve the sugar.

2. Cut the top and bottom off of the pineapple and rinse it well. Cut it into 4-inch pieces, leaving the skin on. Place the chopped pineapple in the warm liquid and turn off the heat.

3. Strain the liquid into a bowl. Place the pineapple in a large, sterilized 3- to 4-gallon glass jar or vessel and add the remaining water along with the warm syrup and spices. Use a fermentation weight to keep the pineapple submerged in the liquid and cover the container with cheesecloth. Secure the cheesecloth with a rubber band or tie.

4. Store the container in a dark, cool place and let it ferment for 4 to 7 days, depending on the time of the year. Hotter months will result in a faster ferment and therefore less time is necessary. Colder months may require 7 days to fully ferment. While wearing a pair of latex gloves, gently stir the contents of the container with your hands each day. Fermenting should begin the second day, and bubbling or foaming inside the container is perfectly normal. You will begin to smell a sweet and sour smell emanating from the mixture.

5. As the fourth day approaches, taste the beverage. It should taste similar to a pineapple mineral water, and should have developed a tiny bit of effervescence. If mold begins to form on the side of the jar at any point, do not drink any of the liquid and discard it.

6. When the tepache is fully fermented and the desired taste has been achieved, strain and enjoy it over ice or store it in the refrigerator.

Mango Lassi

Mangoes, yogurt, water, and sugar are blended together here to make fermented mango lassi, a light and tart beverage that is the height of refreshment.

1 cup plain yogurt

1 cup milk

1 cup ripe mangoes, pits removed, peeled, and chopped

1 tablespoon sugar

½ teaspoon cardamom

1. Place all of the ingredients in a blender and puree until smooth.

2. Pour the puree into a large mason jar and cover the jar with a tight-fitting lid or a cloth secured with a rubber band. Place the jar in a warm, dark place until the flavor has developed to your liking, 12 to 24 hours.

3. Chill the mango lassi in the refrigerator and give it a good shake before enjoying.

Chaas

Chaas is a famous Indian beverage prepared from fermented yogurt and water, commonly referred to on the Subcontinent as "buttermilk" or "chaach," and especially well liked during the hot, muggy summer months there.

1½ cups yogurt

1 teaspoon roasted cumin

1 cup cold water

1 tablespoon chopped fresh mint or cilantro, plus more for garnish

½ teaspoon salt

1. Place the yogurt, cumin, water, mint or cilantro, and salt in a blender and puree for 2 to 3 minutes, until you see a nice, frothy layer with a bit of fat separated from the mixture.

2. Enjoy the chaas immediately, serving it over ice if desired and garnishing with additional herbs, or store it in the refrigerator, where it will keep for a few days.

Sparkling Cider

Combining Champagne yeast with apple juice converts the sugars into alcohol, creating a slightly effervescent and lightly alcoholic beverage.

16 cups apple juice

1 packet of Champagne yeast

1. Place the apple juice and Champagne yeast in a large, sterilized container and stir until thoroughly combined.

2. Cover the container with a cloth or a lid and place it in a warm, dark place until it is bubbly, 7 to 10 days. Check the cider each day to see that it is fermenting properly—if you see any dark, moldy growth, discard the entire mixture and start over with a clean container.

3. Place the sparkling cider in the refrigerator to stop the fermentation. Enjoy chilled or over ice.

Yield: 4 Cups / **Active Time:** 10 Minutes / **Total Time:** 24 to 48 Hours

Kefir

Kefir grains are a blend of yeast and bacteria that, when added to milk, create a sour, lightly carbonated beverage that is rich in probiotics. To make this recipe vegan, you can easily substitute a nondairy milk such as almond milk or coconut milk.

¼ cup kefir grains

4 cups whole milk

1. Place the kefir grains in a large, sterilized jar and add the milk. Cover the jar with a tight-fitting lid or a cloth secured with a rubber band. Place the jar in a warm, dark place and let it ferment until it has thickened and the flavor is tangy, 24 to 48 hours.

2. Strain the kefir through a fine-mesh sieve. Enjoy immediately or store in the refrigerator, where it will keep for up to 1 week.

Kvass

Popular in Eastern Europe, Kvass is a slightly sour and malty drink made from rye bread and various grains or vegetables.

4 cups water

½ cup sugar

2 slices of rye bread

¼ cup raisins (optional)

1. Place the water and sugar in a saucepan and bring to a boil, stirring occasionally to dissolve the sugar.

2. Remove the saucepan from the heat and let the syrup cool to room temperature.

3. Cut the rye bread into small pieces and place them in a large, sterilized mason jar. Add the raisins, if using.

4. Pour the syrup over the bread and seal the jar tightly. Place the jar in a cool, dark place until the flavor of the kvass is slightly sour and malty, and it has a slightly cloudy appearance, 3 to 4 days. Check the jar every day to make sure the kvass is fermenting properly—if you see any dark, moldy growth, discard the entire mixture and start over with a clean mason jar—and to release excess gas from the jar. If the kvass is not sour enough for your liking, let it ferment for a few more days.

5. Chill the kvass in the refrigerator before serving. To serve, dilute it with water to taste. The kvass will keep in the refrigerator for up to 1 week.

Carrot Kvass

Like beets, carrots are a sugary vegetable, and thus a great ingredient to employ as the base of a fermented beverage.

4 cups peeled and grated carrots

1 tablespoon fine sea salt

4 cups water

1. Place the grated carrots and salt in a bowl and massage the salt into the carrots until the carrots start to release their liquid, about 5 minutes.

2. Transfer the carrots to a large, sterilized mason jar, add the water, and seal the jar lightly. Place the jar in a cool, dark place until the flavor of the kvass is slightly sour and sweet, and it has a slightly cloudy appearance, 3 to 4 weeks. Check the jar every few days day to make sure the kvass is fermenting properly—if you see any dark, moldy growth, discard the entire mixture and start over with a clean mason jar—and to release excess gas from the jar. If the kvass is not sour enough for your liking, let it ferment for a few more weeks.

3. Chill the kvass in the refrigerator before serving. To serve, dilute it with water to taste. The kvass will keep in the refrigerator for up to 2 months.

Beet Kvass

The inimitable earthy and sweet flavor of beets was made to be enhanced through fermentation.

4 cups water

2 medium beets, scrubbed and chopped

1 tablespoon fine sea salt

1. Place the water in a saucepan and bring to a boil. Add the beets and salt and reduce the heat so that the water simmers. Cook the beets until they are tender, about 20 minutes.

2. Remove the saucepan from the heat and let the mixture cool to room temperature.

3. Transfer the mixture to a large, sterilized mason jar and seal the jar tightly. Place the jar in a cool, dark place until the flavor of the kvass is slightly sour and earthy, and it has turned a light pink, 3 to 4 weeks. Check the jar every few days day to make sure the kvass is fermenting properly—if you see any dark, moldy growth, discard the entire mixture and start over with a clean mason jar—and to release excess gas from the jar. If the kvass is not sour enough for your liking, let it ferment for a few more weeks.

4. Chill the kvass in the refrigerator before serving. To serve, dilute it with water to taste. The kvass will keep in the refrigerator for up to 2 months.

Beet Kvass

See page 153

Ginger Beer

Store-bought ginger beer is almost always cloyingly sweet. Take control by producing your own at home, and emphasize the spice that the name of the beverage suggests.

4 cups water

1 cup sugar

1 cup grated fresh ginger

1. Place the water in a saucepan and bring it to a boil. Add the sugar and stir until it dissolves. Remove the saucepan from the heat and let the syrup cool to room temperature.

2. Place the ginger in a blender or food processor and puree until it is a smooth paste. Place the ginger paste in a large, sterilized mason jar and add the syrup. Seal the jar tightly and place it in a cool, dark place until the flavor of the ginger beer is spicy and sweet, and it has a slightly cloudy appearance, 3 to 4 weeks. Check the jar every few days day to make sure the ginger is fermenting properly—if you see any dark, moldy growth, discard the entire mixture and start over with a clean mason jar—and to release excess gas from the jar. If the ginger beer is not spicy enough for your liking, add more ginger paste to the jar and let it ferment for another 24 hours.

3. Strain the ginger beer through cheesecloth or a coffee filter and chill in the refrigerator before serving.

Sauces, Vinegars & Condiments

As its true devotees know, the number of dishes that don't benefit from the addition of hot sauce are dwindling by the day. In addition to the addictive spice, there are always numerous levels of flavors lurking within a quality hot sauce, making it an invaluable condiment that can make even a bland preparation seem lively. Incorporating fermentation into a hot sauce takes that complexity to another level, unlocking a unique intensity of flavor.

Another beloved item that hits new heights when live cultures are incorporated is butter. Butter is wonderful on its own, but toning down its sweetness opens up so much more within its creamy confines. Whether you want something special to use as a spread or an ingredient to revolutionize your baking, cultured butter is a true game-changer.

Fermented Hot Sauce

I, like many, am addicted to hot sauce. This particular hot sauce took that addiction to the next level.

2 lbs. cayenne chile peppers

1 lb. jalapeño chile peppers

5 garlic cloves

1 red onion, quartered

3 tablespoons kosher salt, plus more to taste

Filtered water, as needed

1. Remove the tops of the peppers and split them down the middle.

2. Place the split peppers and the garlic, onion, and salt in a sterilized mason jar and cover the mixture with water. Cover the jar and shake well.

3. Place the jar away from direct sunlight and let stand for at least 30 days and up to 6 months—the flavor will improve the longer you let the mixture ferment. Occasionally unscrew the lid to release some of the gases that build up.

4. Once you are ready to make the sauce, reserve most of the brine, transfer the mixture to a blender, and puree to desired thickness. If you want your sauce to be on the thin side, keep adding brine until you have the consistency you want. Season the sauce with salt, transfer to an airtight container, and store in the refrigerator for up to 3 months.

Apple Cider Vinegar

Making apple cider vinegar couldn't be any easier than this. Not only is it delicious but it also prevents food waste by using apple peels and cores.

4 cups apple scraps (peels and cores)

3 tablespoons sugar or cane sugar

3 cups filtered water, plus more as needed

1. Fill a large, sterilized mason jar three-quarters of the way with the apple scraps.

2. Place the sugar and water in a bowl and stir until the sugar has dissolved.

3. Pour the mixture into the mason jar, making sure the liquid covers the apple scraps. If necessary, weigh the apple scraps down with a fermentation weight.

4. Cover the mason jar with cheesecloth and secure with a rubber band or kitchen twine.

5. Store the jar away from direct sunlight and at room temperature for 5 weeks, checking periodically to make sure the apple scraps are covered by liquid. If more liquid is needed, add water to cover.

6. After 5 weeks, strain out the apple scraps and return the liquid to the mason jar. Cover, place away from direct sunlight, and let the mixture sit for another 20 to 30 days.

7. Strain the vinegar before using or storing.

Homemade Miso Paste

This classic Japanese condiment is created by fermenting soybeans with salt and a mold called koji. The result is a paste with a deep, savory flavor that can be used to enhance everything from soups and stir-fries to a Bolognese sauce.

3 cups dried soybeans

3 cups water

½ cup fine sea salt

½ cup brown rice koji

1. Rinse the soybeans and place them in a large pot with the water. Bring the mixture to a boil, reduce the heat to low, and simmer the soybeans until they are tender, 2 to 3 hours.

2. Drain the cooked soybeans and transfer them to a blender. Add the salt and koji and puree until smooth.

3. Transfer the puree to a large mason jar and cover it with a tight-fitting lid. Place the jar in a cool, dark place and let it ferment until the flavor has developed to your liking, 3 to 6 months.

4. Use the miso paste as desired or store it in the refrigerator, where it will keep for up to 1 year.

Mango Vinegar

If you're wondering how many mangoes to purchase to make this deeply flavored vinegar, buy three to make sure you have enough, and make sure they're ripe.

4 cups chopped mangoes

2 cups water

¼ cup white vinegar

¼ cup sugar

1. Place the mangoes in a blender or food processor and puree until smooth.

2. Place the mango puree, water, vinegar, and sugar in a saucepan and bring to a boil, stirring occasionally to dissolve the sugar.

3. Remove the pan from heat and let the mixture cool to room temperature.

4. Transfer the mixture to a large, sterilized mason jar and seal it tightly. Place the jar in a cool, dark place until the flavor of the vinegar is sweet and sour and it has a cloudy appearance, 3 to 4 weeks. Check the jar every few days to make sure the mango vinegar is fermenting properly—if you see any dark, moldy growth, discard the entire mixture and start over with a clean mason jar —and to release excess gas from the jar. If the mango vinegar is not sour enough for your liking, let it ferment for a few more weeks.

5. Use the vinegar immediately or store it in the refrigerator for up to 2 months.

Aam Ka Achar

Sometimes referred to as mango pickles, aam ka achar is a popular Indian condiment that has a distinctive sour and spicy flavor, most often used as a topping for street foods.

1 tablespoon mustard seeds

1 teaspoon fennel seeds

1 teaspoon cumin seeds

1 teaspoon coriander seeds

1 teaspoon coarse sea salt

1 teaspoon sugar

1 lb. mangoes, pits removed, peeled, and chopped

1 cup filtered water

½ cup white vinegar

1. Place the mustard seeds, fennel seeds, cumin seeds, coriander seeds, salt, and sugar in a bowl and stir until combined.

2. Place the mangoes in a large mason jar and sprinkle the spice mixture over the top.

3. Add the water and vinegar to the jar, making sure the mangoes are completely submerged.

4. Cover the jar with a tight-fitting lid or a cloth secured with a rubber band and place the jar in a warm, dark place until the flavor has developed to your liking, 7 to 10 days.

5. Use immediately or store the sauce in the refrigerator.

Aam Ka Achar

See page 167

Kombucha Syrup

A great syrup to use in cocktails, or over ice cream and other desserts.

1 cup sugar

6 cups kombucha

1. Place the sugar and kombucha in a medium saucepan and bring the mixture to a boil.

2. Reduce the heat to medium-low and cook until the syrup has reduced to the desired consistency.

3. Remove the pan from heat and let the syrup cool completely before using or storing in the refrigerator.

Fermented Red Pepper & Garlic Spread

Peppers and garlic both have a natural sweetness that becomes wonderful when countered by the tang supplied by fermentation.

1 lb. red bell peppers, stems and seeds removed, chopped

1 lb. red jalapeño chile peppers, stems and seeds removed, chopped

Cloves from 1 head of garlic

1 tablespoon coarse sea salt

1 cup filtered water

1. Place the peppers, garlic, and salt in a blender and puree until smooth.

2. Transfer the puree to a large jar and press down on it firmly with a wooden spoon to remove any air pockets.

3. Add the water to the jar, making sure that the pepper puree is completely submerged.

4. Cover the jar with a tight-fitting lid or a cloth secured with a rubber band and place the jar in a warm, dark place until the flavor has developed to your liking, 7 to 10 days.

5. Use immediately or store the spread in the refrigerator for up to 2 weeks.

Fermented Red Pepper & Garlic Spread

See page 171

Cultured Butter

Once you try cultured butter, you will never use any other kind of butter again. Why? It is butter that is mixed with yogurt and slightly fermented. What you get is a butter that has beneficial bacteria and a sweet, slightly sour, rich butter flavor.

4 cups high-quality heavy cream

½ cup whole milk yogurt

½ teaspoon kosher salt

1. Place the heavy cream and yogurt in a jar. Seal it and shake vigorously to combine.

2. Open the jar, cover it with cheesecloth, and secure it with a rubber band or kitchen twine.

3. Place the mixture away from direct sunlight and let it sit at room temperature for 36 hours.

4. After 36 hours, seal the jar and place it in the refrigerator for 4 to 6 hours.

5. Remove the mixture from the refrigerator and pour it into the work bowl of a stand mixer fitted with the whisk attachment. Add the salt and whip on high, covering with a towel to prevent spilling, until the butter separates from the buttermilk. Reserve the buttermilk for another preparation.

6. Transfer the butter to a piece of cheesecloth and squeeze out any excess liquid. Wash the butter under ice-cold water and store in an airtight container. It will keep in the refrigerator for approximately 3 months.

Rosemary Cultured Butter

Fans of steak would be wise to add a few knobs of this to the pan and spoon it over the steaks during the last stages of cooking.

4 cups high-quality heavy cream

½ cup whole milk yogurt

4 teaspoons finely chopped fresh rosemary

½ teaspoon kosher salt

1. Place the heavy cream, yogurt, and rosemary in a jar. Seal it and shake vigorously to combine.

2. Open the jar, cover it with cheesecloth, and secure it with a rubber band or kitchen twine.

3. Place the mixture away from direct sunlight and let it sit at room temperature for 36 hours.

4. After 36 hours, seal the jar and place it in the refrigerator for 4 to 6 hours.

5. Remove the mixture from the refrigerator and pour it into the work bowl of a stand mixer fitted with the whisk attachment. Add the salt and whip on high, covering with a towel to prevent spilling, until the butter separates from the buttermilk. Reserve the buttermilk for another preparation.

6. Transfer the butter to a piece of cheesecloth and squeeze out any excess liquid. Wash the butter under ice-cold water and store in an airtight container. It will keep in the refrigerator for approximately 3 months.

Thyme Cultured Butter

Locking the earthy and fresh flavor of thyme into a rich cultured butter makes for a memorable addition to a charcuterie board.

4 cups high-quality heavy cream

½ cup whole milk yogurt

4 teaspoons fresh thyme

½ teaspoon kosher salt

1. Place the heavy cream, yogurt, and thyme in a jar. Seal it and shake vigorously to combine.

2. Open the jar, cover it with cheesecloth, and secure it with a rubber band or kitchen twine.

3. Place the mixture away from direct sunlight and let it sit at room temperature for 36 hours.

4. After 36 hours, seal the jar and place it in the refrigerator for 4 to 6 hours.

5. Remove the mixture from the refrigerator and pour it into the work bowl of a stand mixer fitted with the whisk attachment. Add the salt and whip on high, covering with a towel to prevent spilling, until the butter separates from the buttermilk. Reserve the buttermilk for another preparation.

6. Transfer the butter to a piece of cheesecloth and squeeze out any excess liquid. Wash the butter under ice-cold water and store in an airtight container. It will keep in the refrigerator for approximately 3 months.

Lemon Cultured Butter

Lemon brightens the flavor of butter just enough to allow its richness to really hit home.

4 cups high-quality heavy cream

½ cup whole milk yogurt

1 tablespoon lemon zest

½ teaspoon kosher salt

1. Place the heavy cream, yogurt, and lemon zest in a jar. Seal it and shake vigorously to combine.

2. Open the jar, cover it with cheesecloth, and secure it with a rubber band or kitchen twine.

3. Place the mixture away from direct sunlight and let it sit at room temperature for 36 hours.

4. After 36 hours, seal the jar and place it in the refrigerator for 4 to 6 hours.

5. Remove the mixture from the refrigerator and pour it into the work bowl of a stand mixer fitted with the whisk attachment. Add the salt and whip on high, covering with a towel to prevent spilling, until the butter separates from the buttermilk. Reserve the buttermilk for another preparation.

6. Transfer the butter to a piece of cheesecloth and squeeze out any excess liquid. Wash the butter under ice-cold water and store in an airtight container. It will keep in the refrigerator for approximately 3 months.

Basil Cultured Butter

For those mornings where you need a bit of a treat to face the day, consider spreading this on some toast and then topping it with the Blueberry & Chia Jam (see page 51).

4 cups high-quality heavy cream

½ cup whole milk yogurt

4 teaspoons finely chopped fresh basil

½ teaspoon kosher salt

1. Place the heavy cream, yogurt, and basil in a jar. Seal it and shake vigorously to combine.

2. Open the jar, cover it with cheesecloth, and secure it with a rubber band or kitchen twine.

3. Place the mixture away from direct sunlight and let it sit at room temperature for 36 hours.

4. After 36 hours, seal the jar and place it in the refrigerator for 4 to 6 hours.

5. Remove the mixture from the refrigerator and pour it into the work bowl of a stand mixer fitted with the whisk attachment. Add the salt and whip on high, covering with a towel to prevent spilling, until the butter separates from the buttermilk. Reserve the buttermilk for another preparation.

6. Transfer the butter to a piece of cheesecloth and squeeze out any excess liquid. Wash the butter under ice-cold water and store in an airtight container. It will keep in the refrigerator for approximately 3 months.

Basil Cultured Butter

See page 181

Peach Hot Sauce

Heat is the leading characteristic of this sauce, but the addition of peaches gives it a nice, round sweetness that will work well on pork or chicken.

2 lbs. cayenne chile peppers

1 lb. jalapeño chile peppers

1 lb. peaches, pitted, peeled, and chopped

5 garlic cloves

1 red onion, quartered

3 tablespoons kosher salt, plus more to taste

Filtered water, as needed

1. Remove the tops of the peppers and split them down the middle.

2. Place the split peppers and the peaches, garlic, onion, and salt in a large, sterilized mason jar and cover the mixture with water. Cover the jar and shake well.

3. Place the jar away from direct sunlight and let it stand for at least 30 days and up to 6 months—the flavor will improve the longer you let the mixture ferment. Occasionally unscrew the lid to release some of the gases that build up.

4. Once you are ready to make the sauce, reserve most of the brine, transfer the mixture to a blender, and puree to desired thickness. If you want your sauce to be on the thin side, keep adding brine until you have the consistency you want. Season the sauce with salt, transfer to an airtight container, and store in the refrigerator for up to 3 months.

Sriracha Sauce

Stop heading to the store for this ubiquitous sauce. Making your own at home and allowing it to ferment produces an unbeatable version.

1 lb. red jalapeño chile peppers, stems and seeds removed, chopped

Cloves from 1 head of garlic

1 teaspoon coarse sea salt

1 teaspoon sugar

1 cup filtered water

1 tablespoon white vinegar

1. Place the peppers, garlic, salt, and sugar in a blender and puree until smooth.

2. Transfer the puree to a large jar and press down on it firmly with a wooden spoon to remove any air pockets.

3. Add the water and vinegar to the jar and stir to incorporate, making sure that the pepper puree is completely submerged.

4. Cover the jar with a tight-fitting lid or a cloth secured with a rubber band and place the jar in a warm, dark place until the flavor has developed to your liking, 7 to 10 days.

5. Use immediately or store the sauce in the refrigerator.

Sriracha Sauce

See page 185

Scotch Bonnet Hot Sauce

Yes, scotch bonnet peppers are hot, but in my opinion they are the most flavorful peppers around.

2 lbs. scotch bonnet chile peppers

1 lb. jalapeño chile peppers

5 garlic cloves

1 red onion, quartered

3 tablespoons kosher salt, plus more to taste

Filtered water, as needed

1. Remove the tops of the peppers and split them down the middle.

2. Place the split peppers and the garlic, onion, and salt in a large, sterilized mason jar and cover the mixture with water. Cover the jar and shake well.

3. Place the jar away from direct sunlight and let it stand for at least 30 days and up to 6 months—the flavor will improve the longer you let the mixture ferment. Occasionally unscrew the lid to release some of the gases that build up.

4. Once you are ready to make the sauce, reserve most of the brine, transfer the mixture to a blender, and puree to the desired thickness. If you want your sauce to be on the thin side, keep adding brine until you have the consistency you want. Season the sauce with salt, transfer to an airtight container, and store in the refrigerator for up to 3 months.

Mango & Chile Sauce

Adding the unique, multifaceted flavor of mangoes to a hot sauce makes for a unique sauce.

1 lb. red jalapeño chile peppers, stems and seeds removed, chopped

1 lb. ripe mangoes, pits removed, peeled, and chopped

Cloves from 1 head of garlic

1 teaspoon coarse sea salt

1 teaspoon sugar

1 cup filtered water

1 tablespoon white vinegar

1. Place the peppers, mangoes, garlic, salt, and sugar in a blender and puree until smooth.

2. Transfer the puree to a large jar and press down on it firmly with a wooden spoon to remove any air pockets.

3. Add the water and vinegar to the jar and stir to incorporate, making sure that the pepper puree is completely submerged.

4. Cover the jar with a tight-fitting lid or a cloth secured with a rubber band and place the jar in a warm, dark place until the flavor has developed to your liking, 7 to 10 days.

5. Use immediately or store the sauce in the refrigerator.

Mango & Chile Sauce

See page 189

Mango Hot Sauce

If you can find them, use Alphonso mangoes here, as they have a mind-blowing flavor that blends the best aspects of numerous fruits, from apricots and peaches to melons and citrus.

2 lbs. cayenne chile peppers

1 lb. jalapeño chile peppers

1 lb. mangoes, pitted, peeled, and chopped

1 lb. peaches, pitted, peeled, and chopped

4 garlic cloves

1 red onion, quartered

3 tablespoons kosher salt, plus more to taste

1 teaspoon sugar

Filtered water, as needed

1. Remove the tops of the peppers and split them down the middle.

2. Place the split peppers and the mangoes, peaches, garlic, onion, salt, and sugar in a large, sterilized mason jar and cover the mixture with water. Cover the jar and shake well.

3. Place the jar away from direct sunlight and let stand for at least 30 days and up to 6 months—the flavor will improve the longer you let the mixture ferment. Occasionally unscrew the lid to release some of the gases that build up.

4. Once you are ready to make the sauce, reserve most of the brine, transfer the mixture to a blender, and puree to the desired thickness. If you want your sauce to be on the thin side, keep adding brine until you have the consistency you want. Season the sauce with salt, transfer to an airtight container, and store in the refrigerator for up to 3 months.

Strawberry Hot Sauce

The best part of spring isn't winter being over, but knowing I can replenish my stock of this sweet and bright sauce.

2 lbs. cayenne chile peppers

1 lb. jalapeño chile peppers

1 lb. strawberries, hulled

1 lb. peaches, pitted, peeled, and chopped

4 garlic cloves

1 red onion, quartered

3 tablespoons kosher salt, plus more to taste

1 teaspoon sugar

Filtered water, as needed

1. Remove the tops of the peppers and split them down the middle.

2. Place the split peppers and the strawberries, peaches, garlic, onion, salt, and sugar in a large, sterilized mason jar and cover the mixture with water. Cover the jar and shake well.

3. Place the jar away from direct sunlight and let stand for at least 30 days and up to 6 months—the flavor will improve the longer you let the mixture ferment. Occasionally unscrew the lid to release some of the gases that build up.

4. Once you are ready to make the sauce, reserve most of the brine, transfer the mixture to a blender, and puree to desired thickness. If you want your sauce to be on the thin side, keep adding brine until you have the consistency you want. Season the sauce with salt, transfer to an airtight container, and store in the refrigerator for up to 3 months.

Insanely Hot Hot Sauce

Like it extrememly hot? This one is for you. Just don't forget that I warned you.

2 lbs. cayenne chile peppers

1 lb. jalapeño chile peppers

½ lb. scotch bonnet chile peppers

6 garlic cloves

1 red onion, quartered

¼ cup kosher salt, plus more to taste

Filtered water, as needed

1. Remove the tops of the peppers and split them down the middle.

2. Place the split peppers and the garlic, onion, and salt in a large, sterilized mason jar and cover the mixture with water. Cover the jar and shake well.

3. Place the jar away from direct sunlight and let stand for at least 30 days and up to 6 months—the flavor will improve the longer you let the mixture ferment. Occasionally unscrew the lid to release some of the gases that build up.

4. Once you are ready to make the sauce, reserve most of the brine, transfer the mixture to a blender, and puree to desired thickness. If you want your sauce to be on the thin side, keep adding brine until you have the consistency you want. Season the sauce with salt, transfer to an airtight container, and store in the refrigerator for up to 3 months.

Metric Conversions

U.S. Measurement	Approximate Metric Liquid Measurement	Approximate Metric Dry Measurement
1 teaspoon	5 ml	—
1 tablespoon or ½ ounce	15 ml	14 g
1 ounce or ⅛ cup	30 ml	29 g
¼ cup or 2 ounces	60 ml	57 g
⅓ cup	80 ml	—
½ cup or 4 ounces	120 ml	113 g
⅔ cup	160 ml	—
¾ cup or 6 ounces	180 ml	—
1 cup or 8 ounces or ½ pint	240 ml	227 g
1½ cups or 12 ounces	350 ml	—
2 cups or 1 pint or 16 ounces	475 ml	454 g
3 cups or 1½ pints	700 ml	—
4 cups or 2 pints or 1 quart	950 ml	—

Index

Acknowledgments

Jitti Chaithiraphant

Your passion for the art of fermentation inspired me so many years ago. My life has been filled with knowledge because of your friendship. Thank you for everything. It's been an honor learning from you all these years.

William J. Dunkerley

Thank you for inspiring so many in the New Hampshire chef community to forage and ferment. It's been an honor to call you friend and learn from you. I am so proud of the man, businessman, and friend you are.

About the Author

Keith Sarasin is an author, chef, speaker, and restaurateur. In 2012, Keith started The Farmers Dinner. Since 2012, The Farmers Dinner has hosted over 100 farm-to-table events across New England, fed more than 19,000 customers, and raised over $188,000 for local farms.

In addition, Keith has studied Indian food and history for the last 10 years, which led him to starting Aatma. Aatma is an exciting and unique tasting experience that presents food from the Indian subcontinent with modern techniques and styles.

Keith is the author of four other books, *The Perfect Turkey*, *The Farmers Dinner Cookbook*, *Meat: The Ultimate Cookbook*, and *Jerky: The Essential Cookbook*. For more on Keith and his work, follow him on Instagram (@keithsarasin) or visit his website, keithsarasin.com.

About Cider Mill Press Book Publishers

Good ideas ripen with time. From seed to harvest,
Cider Mill Press brings fine reading, information, and entertainment together
between the covers of its creatively crafted books. Our Cider Mill bears fruit
twice a year, publishing a new crop of titles each spring and fall.

"Where Good Books Are Ready for Press"

501 Nelson Place
Nashville, TN 37214
cidermillpress.com